AF488192

THE IMPACT LEADERS

A COLLECTION OF STORIES FROM THE GLOBAL CHANGE MAKERS

FEATURING KEVIN HARRINGTON AND GLOBAL AUTHORS OF THE INTERNATIONAL IMPACT BOOK AWARDS

CONTENTS

INTRODUCTION

THE STORY BEHIND THE STORIES

When I first met Kevin Harrington, the original *Shark Tank* investor and one of the most iconic names in modern entrepreneurship, I had no idea that moment would become the catalyst for something so impactful.

Our connection wasn't built around transactions. It was built on transformation.

Kevin has spent his life helping bold thinkers bring ideas to life. I've spent mine helping authors bring their stories into the spotlight. We came from different worlds, but shared one unwavering belief: **when people step up to share their truth, they don't just change their lives, they change the world around them.**

That belief is the heartbeat of this book.

The Impact Leaders isn't just a collection of stories, it's a movement. A movement of modern-day visionaries who have turned pain into purpose, obstacles into opportunities, and their message into a mission.

Each chapter in this book holds the journey of someone who decided to stand in their truth and lead with courage. These are not perfect people. They're not distant icons on a pedestal. They are people just like you and me, people who chose to rise above the noise, show up for others, and serve with heart.

And now, they're letting you in on their journey. Their wisdom. Their strategy. Their impact.

As someone who came from humble beginnings in a part of the world where women weren't always taught to dream big, I understand the power of a single decision to change everything. The decision to speak. To write. To lead. And most importantly, to believe that your story is worth telling.

This book is here to remind you: **you don't need permission to lead. Your story is your calling card.**

Whether you are an entrepreneur, a creative, a community leader, or simply someone with a fire in your soul—you'll find something in these pages that reminds you of who you are and what you're capable of.

I'm deeply honored to collaborate with Kevin Harrington and every author featured in this book. Their insights are raw, real, and rooted in impact.

So turn the page. Let their stories fuel your own. And remember—
This isn't just a book.

This is your invitation to rise.

With all my heart,

Nim Stant
Founder, International Impact Book Awards

BUILDING IMPACT FROM THE GROUND UP

BY KEVIN HARRINGTON

ORIGINAL SHARK ON SHARK TANK, INVENTOR OF THE INFOMERCIAL, & CO-FOUNDER OF BIG BRAND VENTURES

When I think of *Impact leadership,* here's what comes to mind. I believe it's about creating fast, meaningful growth that leaves a lasting mark. I've been known to call it "Quantum Entrepreneurship," which means building businesses that SCALE fast.

My journey in entrepreneurship began in the mid-1980s with the Small Business Center in Cincinnati, Ohio. It was a one-stop shop for entrepreneurs where I brokered deals, sold businesses, and learned from the inside out how companies operate. That experience gave me front-row access to hundreds of financial records, negotiations, and owner struggles. What I learned was that real impact comes from solving problems at scale and finding ways to multiply opportunities for others.

That mindset eventually led me to launch products like the *Ginsu Knife*, Tony Little's Target Training DVDs, Jack LaLanne's Juicer, and more! I didn't invent these products. I had a gift for spotting opportunities, packaging them the right way, and building systems to scale. Over the years, those instincts created billions in sales, dozens of global brands, and opportunities for entrepreneurs all over the world.

The good news is that none of this is magic, but rather a process. After 40+ years of wins, losses, and Shark Tank pitches, I've narrowed it down to seven key steps.

Step 1: Exercise Curiosity

The first step to impactful growth is curiosity. You can't build big if you're not constantly exposing yourself to new industries, products, and people.

For me, this started at trade shows. That's where I met Arnold Morris, who could slice through a Coca-Cola can and still cut a tomato with the same knife. Arnold was magnetic, and I thought, *What if we filmed this pitch and aired it on TV?* That idea led to the iconic *Ginsu Knife* infomercial and $500 million in sales.

From there, I started seeking out others like Billy Mays, Tony Little, Jack LaLanne, and George Foreman. Every one of them had raw intellectual property (a fitness method, a daily habit, a slanted grill) that just needed to be unpacked, productized, and shared with the world. Curiosity opened the door.

Today, curiosity overload doesn't just mean walking trade show floors. It means watching digital trends, analyzing what's hot on QVC, Kickstarter, or TikTok, and constantly scanning the horizon for the next wave.

Step 2: Create a Powerful Foundation

Fast growth without a plan is chaos. I've seen entrepreneurs dump $300,000 into an idea without a business plan, only to wonder why investors won't call back.

Your blueprint is your map. This could include an executive summary, competitive analysis, sales channels, marketing plan, and clear metrics. In my world, there are two numbers that matter most… Customer Acquisition Cost (CAC), which is how much you pay to get a customer. Secondly, Average Order Value (AOV) is how much each customer spends.

Push acquisition costs down, push order value up, and you've got a scalable business! Without this blueprint, you're driving fast with no guidance.

Step 3: Raise Smart Capital

The truth is, you likely can't grow a business to $100 million without outside capital. Over the past 40 years, I've raised well over $1 billion across my ventures, and the key is knowing your investors' sweet spot.

Some investors want profits. Others want fast user growth, even if it means losing money for years. On Shark Tank, Kevin O'Leary loves royalties, and Barbara Corcoran loves real estate angles. Understanding what excites your investor is the difference between getting a check or getting rejected.

Sometimes, the capital is hiding in plain sight. I once raised $2 million just by getting advances from my manufacturer, media buyers, and industry suppliers who wanted exclusivity. That's a great example of creative financing.

Step 4: Build Your Dream Team

I learned this lesson the hard way. I once invested half a million into a Shark Tank entrepreneur who had passion, but no operational or finance team. Six months later, the money was gone.

Great businesses are orchestras, not solo acts. You should bring in mentors, seasoned executives, and partners with exits under their belt. When I launched a beauty company, I brought in the former President of L'Oréal. He didn't cost me millions; however, he got equity and a seat at the table.

If you don't build your dream team, you're building your dream problem!

Step 5: Master the Perfect Pitch

Every product, business, and investment lives or dies by the pitch. Over the years, I've developed a simple formula… "Tease, Please, and Seize."

Tease with an attention-grabbing problem (like the Ginsu Knife cutting through a Coca-Cola can). **Please** with the solution and irresistible benefits. And lastly, **seize** with a compelling offer that forces action.

On Shark Tank, I've seen hundreds of pitches. Most fail because they lack emotional connection. One entrepreneur broke down crying while telling her story, and the producers told Kevin O'Leary to hold back, because emotion sells. People buy stories, not spreadsheets.

Step 6: Raise Your Profile

In all honesty, in today's world, if you're not seen, you don't exist. That's why I've spent decades raising my profile and personal brand through media tours, radio, books, podcasts, and, eventually, Shark Tank.

Authority builds trust, testimonials build credibility, and editorial coverage builds momentum. The right press tour can take a $1 million idea and turn it into a $10 million business. Just ask Rebecca Rescate, who pitched me *City Kitty* (a cat toilet-training kit). With press exposure, that quirky product did $10 million in sales.

Step 7: Partner for Growth

The fastest way to scale is through partnerships. I didn't invent the products I sold. Instead, I partnered with inventors, suppliers, distributors, and media giants.

When I wanted to launch a mobile app, I didn't start from scratch. I partnered with Sprint, which preloaded my app on millions of phones. That's an example of distribution leverage. In a world shifting to mobile-first and app-driven engagement, partnerships are more powerful than ever. They give you instant access to customers, credibility, and cash flow.

THE IMPACT LEGACY

Looking back, what I'm most proud of isn't the billions in sales, it's the ripple effect. Endeavors like helping Tony Little turn fitness into a household name or helping Jack LaLanne inspire health in millions of homes. Giving entrepreneurs their first big break on Shark Tank has always been so important.

Impact leadership is more than money. It's about creating opportunities, mentoring the next generation, and using your platform to open doors for others. My father (my first mentor) taught me that "success is temporary, but impact lasts forever."

Everything I've built, from creating shows to launching companies to investing in ideas, started with putting myself out there, telling my story, and taking consistent action when nobody was watching. Back when I was door-to-door selling, I didn't know who was paying attention. But those early days of grinding, sharing my journey, and being willing to evolve laid the foundation for everything that came after.

Today, as the co-founder of Big Brand Ventures, I've taken everything I've learned and built a company focused on scaling brands and helping entrepreneurs turn their vision into reality. We work with businesses that want more than quick wins, and we partner with leaders who are building for long-term growth, sustainability, and legacy. Big Brand Ventures is the culmination of numerous decades of experience.

So, remember to grow fast, build wisely, and leave the world better than you found it!

KEVIN HARRINGTON

An original "shark" on the hit TV show Shark Tank, the creator of the infomercial, pioneer of the As Seen on TV brand, and cofounding board member of the Entrepreneur's Organization— Kevin Harrington has pushed past all the questions and excuses to repeatedly enjoy 100X success.

His legendary work behind the scenes of business ventures has produced well over $5 billion in global sales, the launch of more than 500 products, and the making of dozens of millionaires. Twenty of his companies have each topped $100 million in revenue. Through his entrepreneurial experiences, Kevin realized his talent for turning underutilized assets into growth opportunities.

While watching late-night television, he realized nothing was being broadcast on the Discovery Channel after normal broadcast hours. He seized the opportunity to launch what later came to be called the infomercial. Before long, he had helped make "but wait, there's more" part of our cultural history.

He's launched massively successful products like The Food Saver, Ginsu Knives, The Great Wok of China, The Flying Lure, and many more.

He has worked with amazing celebrities like Billie Mays, Tony Little, Jack Lalanne, and George Foreman, to name a few. Kevin then built on that success to help pioneer the As Seen on TV brand. After empowering others to achieve success, he recognized the shifting marketplace trends and began to intentionally build his personal brand.

www.KevinHarrington.tv

THE NEW RULES OF IMPACT: WHAT IT REALLY MEANS TO LEAD TODAY

BY NIM STANT

FOUNDER & CEO OF THE INTERNATIONAL IMPACT BOOK AWARDS, & TV HOST OF THE GLOBAL THOUGHT LEADERS ON ABC15

I didn't grow up with Hollywood lights or Silicon Valley startups in my backyard. I grew up in Thailand, where survival, not strategy, was the first skill you learned. I didn't dream of becoming a CEO or hosting red carpet galas. I dreamed of having enough: enough food, enough freedom, enough voice to make choices without asking permission.

At twenty-one, I left my home with nothing but a backpack and one irrational belief that maybe, just maybe, I was made for something more. I didn't speak English. I didn't know the rules. I had no roadmap or backup plan. But life in the jungle, both literal and metaphorical, taught me something that would shape my future: if you hesitate, the world will decide for you. If you act, you get to shape your own destiny.

Life tested that lesson hard. I became a solo mom of two. I worked long days teaching yoga in five different studios, driving from one side of town to the other in a beat-up car, piecing together just enough to keep us afloat. I would show up smiling for my students, only to cry in the car between classes, exhausted and unsure how I would make it to the end of the week. There was no audience clapping for me. No cameras. No applause. Just the quiet decision day after day to keep going.

That's the truth no one sees when they see me today: the founder of the International Impact Book Awards, the host of television shows, the producer of documentaries, the woman building stages in Hollywood for authors and entrepreneurs. They see the spotlight. But they don't see the darkness I had to walk through to get here.

And that's where real leadership begins.

Leadership isn't a title. It isn't something handed to you once you've "made it." It isn't the photo on the cover of a magazine, or the award on your shelf. **Leadership is the choice to keep moving forward when no one is watching. It's the choice to impact others even when you feel like you have nothing left to give.**

The world is full of people chasing titles. CEO. Founder. Influencer. Bestselling Author. But none of those matter if you haven't first chosen to lead with impact. Because titles fade. Followers disappear. But the difference you make in another person's life that outlasts you.

Here's what I've learned: real leadership begins in the quiet moments, not the loud ones. It begins when you stay disciplined even when no one's keeping score. When you choose honesty over approval. When you decide to build something that serves others, not just yourself.

This is the foundation of impact. And this is the heartbeat of the new rules of leadership.

Today, the world doesn't just need more leaders, it needs **impact leaders.**

An impact leader isn't the person with the most followers, the fanciest title, or the loudest voice in the room. An impact leader is the person who shows up, consistently and authentically, with a message that matters. Someone who doesn't just speak about change but creates it, first in their own life, and then in the lives of others.

That's why I built platforms like the International Impact Book Awards. Because I've seen over and over again that the people who make the biggest difference aren't always the ones with the biggest platforms. They are the people willing to step out, share their truth, and serve with courage.

And that's why I wrote this chapter. To teach you that leadership isn't about being perfect, fearless, or famous. It's about being intentional, authentic, and willing to go first. It's about understanding that your story isn't just about you, it's about who you can inspire, what movements you can ignite, and what legacy you can leave behind.

So let's redefine leadership. Let's dispel the myth that it's reserved for the powerful or the privileged. Let's talk about what it really means to create impact and how you, right now, can start leading in a way that matters.

Because here's the truth: leadership isn't a title. **Leadership is a choice.** And when you choose to lead with impact, you don't just change your life, you change the world around you.

WHAT IT MEANS TO BE A REAL LEADER

For too long, leadership has been defined by position. The corner office. The job title. The microphone. The spotlight. We've been conditioned to believe that you're not a "leader" until someone hands you authority or declares you important enough to follow.

But here's the truth: **leadership isn't about position. It's about responsibility.**

It's the responsibility to serve, to speak, to make decisions that ripple out beyond yourself. You don't need a title to do that. You don't need a company card or a million followers. You just need the courage to step forward and own the impact of your choices.

THE OLD MODEL VS. IMPACT LEADERSHIP

The old model of leadership thrived on fear, hierarchy, and authority. Power flowed downward. Leaders demanded respect because of their title, not because of their actions. And in many ways, this model worked for its time. Factories ran. Armies marched. Companies grew.

But in today's world, that model is broken. People no longer follow titles, they follow trust. They don't stay loyal to hierarchies; they stay loyal to humans. Influence is no longer inherited; it's earned.

That's where **impact leadership** comes in.

Impact leadership is built on service, courage, and story. It's leadership that doesn't push people from above, it pulls people forward. It's not about how loudly you command, but how deeply you connect.

The most powerful leaders I know embody this.

Take Kevin Harrington, the original Shark from *Shark Tank*. Kevin didn't build his empire by hiding behind titles. He built it by creating opportunities by listening to entrepreneurs, by seeing potential before anyone else did, and by investing in people's stories. His leadership isn't about celebrity. It's about scale helping others multiply their impact.

Or Sharon Lechter, co-author of *Rich Dad Poor Dad*. Sharon's leadership came not from chasing the spotlight, but from teaching financial literacy to millions who had been ignored by the system. She turned her book into a movement by serving with clarity and conviction. She didn't just build wealth; she built wisdom into generations.

And then there's Brené Brown. She didn't take the stage because she was fearless. She took the stage because she was willing to be vulnerable about shame, imperfection, and courage. Her TED Talk has been viewed more than 60 million times, not because she "had all the answers," but because she gave us permission to be human. That is impact leadership changing the way the world talks about something by having the courage to go first.

THE FOUR PILLARS OF IMPACT LEADERSHIP

After years of building my own platforms, interviewing leaders, and mentoring authors, I've come to see that impact leadership always rests on four pillars: **Story, Service, Strategy, and Scale.**

1. **Story:** Your story is the foundation of your leadership. It's not your resume or your credentials that inspire people, it's your journey, your scars, your lessons. Leaders don't hide their story; they use it to build bridges of trust.

   Practical takeaway: Write down three defining moments in your life. Ask: *How does this connect to the people I want to serve? How can my story become their permission slip?*

2. **Service:** Leadership isn't about being at the top it's about putting yourself in the place where you can serve most effectively. The best leaders I know are obsessed with solving problems for others, not just promoting themselves.

   Practical takeaway: List out the top three challenges your audience faces. Then ask: *How can I use my expertise or platform to remove one of these barriers for them?*

3. **Strategy:** Intentions matter, but execution matters more. Impact leaders don't just inspire people emotionally; they build systems, processes, and models that create real change. Without strategy, leadership is just a pep talk.

   Practical takeaway: Map your next 90 days. What is one concrete project that will move your mission forward? Break it into weekly steps and commit.

4. **Scale:** Leadership that ends with you is limited. True impact multiplies. That means creating books, podcasts, documentaries, or platforms that allow your voice to live beyond your presence. Scale ensures your story keeps working, even when you're not in the room.

   Practical takeaway: Choose one way to scale your message in the next year: a book, a podcast, a course, or a live event. Commit to building one platform that amplifies your leadership.

WHY THIS MATTERS FOR ENTREPRENEURS

If you're building a business, these four pillars aren't optional, they're essential. In a world flooded with noise, entrepreneurs who lead with stories stand out. Those who lead with service build loyal customers. Those who commit to strategy see measurable results. And those who embrace scale create movements that outlive a single product or launch.

Leadership is no longer about being in charge; it's about being responsible. About taking your story, aligning it with service, anchoring it in strategy, and multiplying it through scale.

That is what it means to be an Impact Leader.

WHAT IT MEANS TO CREATE AN IMPACT

If leadership is responsibility, then impact is the result. It's what happens when your choices, your story, and your strategy ripple beyond your own life and start shaping the lives of others.

At the International Impact Book Awards, I see this every single day. Authors from around the world send in their work, hoping their story will matter. And when they stand on our red carpet, they're not just holding a book. They're holding a movement in its earliest form. Because books do more than share information, they move culture.

Think about it: some of the greatest cultural shifts in history started with a book. *Silent Spring* sparked the environmental movement. *Rich Dad Poor Dad* reshaped how families think about money. Even fiction like *To Kill a Mockingbird* challenged generations to rethink justice and morality. Stories are not passive. They are the blueprints that give people permission to think, act, and believe differently.

That's why, at the International Impact Book Awards, we don't just celebrate winners—we celebrate every author. Because the truth is, everyone wins when a story is shared. Every voice matters. Every book has the potential to spark change.

CASE STUDIES: STORIES THAT SPARKED MORE

I've watched authors transform their books into entire ecosystems of influence.

One author turned her memoir of survival into a nonprofit that supports women leaving abusive relationships. Another used his business book as the foundation for a coaching company, teaching entrepreneurs around the world how to scale with discipline. I've seen children's authors create merchandise lines and school programs, building entire communities around their characters.

These authors didn't stop at publishing. They engineered impact through **visibility** and **platforms.** They treated their books not as a diary entry, but as a **blueprint for others.**

Impact doesn't happen by accident. It's created when you build the right systems around your story. It's built when you decide your book is not the finish line, but the launchpad.

MY STORY: FROM PAIN TO PLATFORM

Thai Tiger was born out of pain. I didn't write it because I wanted to add another title to my résumé. I wrote it because I needed to make sense of the struggles I had faced growing up in Thailand, moving to the U.S. with nothing, surviving as a solo mom, and building a business against all odds.

But here's what I realized: my story wasn't just therapy. It was a strategy. It wasn't just for me. It was for every entrepreneur who has ever felt underestimated. For every woman who has ever been told to "stay small." For every dreamer who wondered if their scars disqualified them from success.

That's why Thai Tiger didn't stay in the book. It became a documentary. And then it became the foundation for Nim Stant Productions, a company built to help other authors and entrepreneurs do the same. We don't just produce content. We turn books into films. We turn entrepreneurs into celebrity experts. We create platforms that give people authority, visibility, and credibility in their industries.

That's the essence of impact: when your story becomes more than words. When it transforms into a stage, a screen, a movement. When it multiplies.

THE BLUEPRINT FOR IMPACT

Here's what I've learned:

1. **Impact Starts with Ownership:** You have to stop seeing your story as a private diary entry and start owning it as a public blueprint. Your lessons, your scars, your failures—they're not just personal history. They're raw material for someone else's breakthrough.

2. **Impact Requires Visibility:** A book sitting on your desk doesn't create change. It's when that book is shared through media, podcasts, stages, and red carpets that it starts to influence. Visibility is not vanity; it's responsibility.

3. **Impact Scales through Platforms:** Your book is step one. But what comes next? A workshop? A podcast? A documentary? An online community? If you want lasting influence, you must build platforms that allow your story to outlive you.

4. **Impact Creates Legacy:** When you turn your story into a system that others can learn from, you create ripple effects that go beyond your lifetime. Your book, your business, your brand, they become the inheritance you leave for generations.

WHY THIS MATTERS FOR YOU

Maybe you've been telling yourself your book is "just for you." A personal project. A passion. But let me challenge you: what if it's bigger than that? What if your story could help someone step out of fear? What if your lessons could save someone five years of mistakes? What if your voice could move culture forward?

You don't need to wait for permission. You don't need to wait to "be ready." Impact begins the moment you decide your story is not just about you.

Because here's the truth: **impact happens when you stop seeing your story as a diary entry and start treating it as a blueprint for others.**

That's what I've built my life around. That's why I celebrate authors, produce films, and create stages. Because I believe every story has the power to start a movement if you're brave enough to share it.

So the question isn't whether your story matters. The question is: *Are you ready to use it to create impact?*

POSITIONING YOURSELF AS A MODERN IMPACT LEADER

The landscape of leadership has changed. In the past, leaders relied on titles, hierarchy, or institutions to establish authority. Today, credibility isn't handed down from a corner office or a boardroom. It's earned through visibility, authenticity, and service.

For authors and entrepreneurs, this means your book is not the finish line; it's the launchpad. What you do after your book is published is what determines whether you remain a writer or evolve into an **Impact Leader.**

Here's the truth: you don't wait for someone to put you on a stage. You build the stage.

I've seen this firsthand in my own work. When I created red-carpet galas for authors, it wasn't to chase glamour; it was to prove a principle. Visibility multiplies credibility. Photos, interviews, and media coverage provide authors with assets that elevate their standing in the eyes of clients, investors, and audiences. The gala became more than an event; it became a platform for authors to position themselves as authorities.

When I sat down with thought leaders like Kevin Harrington from *Shark Tank* or stars from *The Secret,* the lesson wasn't about celebrity, it was about proximity. Partnering and aligning yourself with established leaders accelerates trust. It shows your audience that you're part of a larger conversation worth listening to.

And when I launched production projects like *Thai Tiger,* it wasn't about spotlighting my story; it was about showing that a book can live far beyond the page. It can evolve into a documentary, a podcast, or even a movement. Authors often underestimate the depth of their own intellectual property. But the truth is, your story can expand across industries if you position it intentionally.

So what does positioning yourself as a modern Impact Leader look like in practice?

1. **Own Your Story:** Stop hiding the struggles that shaped you. They are the bridge that connects you to others.

2. **Step into Media:** Podcasts, interviews, red-carpet photos, and press features are not vanity. They're assets. Use them.

3. **Partner Up:** Align with mentors, colleagues, or influencers who amplify your message. Borrowed credibility compounds quickly.

4. **Build Your Stage:** If no one is inviting you, create your own podcast, your own summit, or your own book awards. Leadership is the momentum you generate.

The bottom line? Modern leadership isn't about waiting for the world to notice you. It's about showing up consistently, building platforms strategically, and positioning yourself so your voice has weight.

Your story matters. Not one day. Not when it's more polished. Not when it feels safer. It matters now.

Your book is not an ending, it's the beginning of something bigger. It's the blueprint for building a platform, a community, and a legacy. But none of that happens if you leave your story on the shelf.

Leadership doesn't promise comfort. Neither does impact. Both require the willingness to stand when others stay silent, to act when others wait, to keep going when others quit. But if you choose to lead even imperfectly, you create ripples that outlast you.

Here's the truth: movements don't start with institutions, money, or policies. They start with one person bold enough to tell the truth. One voice willing to say, "This is my story, and I know it can serve others."

That voice can be yours.

The jungle doesn't promise safety. Neither does leadership. But if you step forward, if you use your story as both mirror and map, you can ignite change that outlives your lifetime.

Your story is your impact. Your book is your beginning. And your choice to lead is the legacy you leave.

NIM STANT

Nim's work is driven by a deep-seated belief that every story has the power to change lives. She is fervently dedicated to helping authors and entrepreneurs amplify their voices, overcome obstacles, and transform their messages into movements that resonate globally. Through the International Impact Book Awards, she is on a mission to elevate the literary world and empower authors to make a meaningful impact on their audiences.

Nim has had the privilege of working with world-renowned authors and entrepreneurs, including Sharon Lechter, Mark Victor Hansen, Sean Kanan, Brian Tracy, Dr. Joe Vitale, Daymond John, Kevin Harrington, Jeff Fagin, Alex Hormozi, and many more. Her expertise and influence have been recognized globally, with features in over 480 media outlets worldwide.

Nim Stant is an entrepreneur, author, and influencer with an unwavering commitment to unlocking the full potential of the human experience. Born into a broken middle-class family, Nim learned from an early age the power of resilience, determination, and living with purpose. Her journey has been one of transformation, and she has channeled her experiences into a vibrant career dedicated to helping others break free from limiting beliefs, pursue their dreams, and take bold action in their lives.

With over 20 years of experience, Nim's passion for empowering others has only grown stronger. In 2020, she founded the International Impact Book Awards, a groundbreaking initiative that opens doors for independent authors and publishers worldwide.

Through this platform, Nim has cultivated a diverse and dynamic community of literary talent, providing authors with the recognition, support, and resources they need to share their stories and expertise with the world.

www.NimStant.com

BUILD YOUR BRAND & MAXIMIZE IMPACT

BY BRANDON T. ADAMS

CO-CEO OF BIG BRAND VENTURES, EMMY® AWARD-WINNING PRODUCER, & HOST OF "BEYOND SMALL TOWN DREAMS" DOCUMENTARY

If there's one truth I've learned throughout the years as an entrepreneur, it's that becoming an *Impact Leader* isn't about having all the answers. The most impactful thing you can do is Take Massive Action. You have to make that first call, share your story with the world, and surround yourself with people who push you to grow. Action creates momentum, and momentum can change your life.

For me, the constant thread through every season of my career has been the importance of "Building a Brand." Wherever I've been in life, I've always made a point of documenting my journey, sharing it online, and building trust with my audience. Sometimes the right person only needs to see you once. Over the years, I've told countless people, "One view can change your life" because I've lived it.

I've seen firsthand how a strong personal brand can create influence, opportunities, and impact beyond what you could ever imagine. The story I'm about to share is proof that building your personal brand is one of the most powerful investments you will ever make in your career. Once you understand the power of telling your story, you'll realize that your next breakthrough might only be one pivot away.

ROCK BOTTOM

The phone rang, and I'll never forget the tone in my wife's voice. "Brandon, I can't find the vehicle."

It was a cold Minnesota winter, snow covering the parking lot where she stood. I was back home in Garnavillo, Iowa, four hours away at my parents' house. At first, I thought she had just forgotten where she had parked. But deep down, I knew what had happened.

The bank had repossessed it.

That moment hit harder than anything I had ever experienced before. To the outside world, I was "the entrepreneur guy." Constantly speaking on stages, producing shows, and winning awards. But behind the scenes, I was broke, deep in debt, and now facing my wife on the phone, stranded without a car.

I walked into my old bedroom at my parents' house, shut the door, and let the frustration pour out. I promised myself, "**This will never happen again**. I will not be broke. I will turn this around, and one day I'll tell this story to help other people."

I didn't have the exact plan yet, but I made the decision right there. That was my line in the sand.

The truth is, the most important parts of your brand aren't built when everything's going well. They're built in these moments, when you're tested. How you respond when you're at rock bottom shapes the story people will remember.

GROWING UP

Before the repossession, Emmy Awards, and partnerships with people like Kevin Harrington, I was just a kid from a small Iowa farm town with more cornfields than people. My dad ran a packaged ice business, and from the time I could carry a bag, I was helping him load trucks and make deliveries.

We'd spend the day hauling ice to bars, restaurants, grocery stores, and gas stations. My dad knew every customer's name. He shook hands, listened to their stories, and ensured they received exactly what they needed.

It wasn't anything fancy, but it was the best training I could have asked for. I learned how to show up for commitments. It taught me to treat people well, whether they could help me or not. Most importantly, I learned that doing the job right, even when nobody was watching, was non-negotiable. Those early days still drive how I build relationships and run businesses today.

MY FIRST BIG IDEA

The first time I really tried to build something bigger was with an invention called the Arctic Stick. I poured over $100,000 into developing it. However, it didn't achieve the level of success that I originally had in mind. In the end, the lifetime sales were about $10,000.

Most people would call that a failure. And in one way, it was. But it was also the education that set up everything else. I learned how to raise money through **crowdfunding**, how to pitch to investors, how to handle rejection, and how to keep going when people doubted me.

That invention also introduced me to Cactus Jack Barringer, a fellow inventor who had given a pitch on Shark Tank. Jack gave me a book that completely changed my mindset. *Think and Grow Rich* by Napoleon Hill has stuck with me every day since. I realized that success wasn't just about the product or the money. It was about mindset, persistence, and the people you surround yourself with. That's also the foundation of any brand worth building!

By 2015, I was hustling to get the word out about what I was doing. I started a podcast, interviewed entrepreneurs, and drove anywhere I thought there might be an opportunity. Most nights, I slept in my truck. I would shower at LA Fitness and live on $5 footlongs and canned food. No matter the circumstances, I kept going. If you want your brand to stand out, you can't just show up when it's easy. You have to keep showing up when nobody's watching.

THE CONNECTION THAT CHANGED EVERYTHING

One of my early podcast guests was John Lee Dumas from *Entrepreneurs on Fire*. At the end of the interview, I asked him, "How can I help you?" That one question led me to run the crowdfunding campaign for his book, *The Freedom Journal*. We raised $453,000 in 33 days, built three schools for Pencils of Promise, and turned it into a multimillion-dollar launch. That project then caught the attention of Original Shark on *Shark Tank*, Kevin Harrington. Just like that, a single conversation shifted the entire trajectory of my career. This is why I tell people to focus on providing real value first, and then watch as the opportunities follow.

PARTNERING WITH A SHARK

When I met Kevin, I walked away with the start of a real business relationship. I actually hired him to speak at one of my events. I knew that I needed to bring value to him, so that's what I did. Over time, that relationship became a partnership. I learned how he built brands, scaled companies, and led teams. Eventually, we teamed up and co-founded Big Brand Ventures alongside his son Brian Harrington.

Now, we work with companies across industries, helping them scale into the tens and hundreds of millions. However, the main objective has remained the same. It's always been about creating real impact and helping people grow. I've learned that the people you choose to learn from will shape everything you build. After all, you are the average of the five people you spend the most time with!

REDEFINING SUCCESS

Over the years, my definition of success has changed. When I was 15 years old, it was taking a girl on a date! At 25, I was striving to make as much money as possible. At 29, in the middle of a financial collapse, I was figuring out how to keep the lights on. Today, it's about helping people, growing our company, and building something that lasts. My wife Samantha, my niece Jordyn and nephew Jaxon, my parents, my family, and my team are the reason I keep going. Your "why" will evolve over time. If you're building a brand without understanding why it matters to you, it's only a matter of time before you burn out.

THE EMMY MOMENT

In 2018, Samantha and I launched *Success in Your City*. The idea came to us when we were sitting on a beach, and I asked, "Wouldn't it be cool if we traveled the country and interviewed people from all walks of life?"

At first, she thought I was crazy, until we couldn't stop thinking about it. So we did exactly that. *Success in Your City* was a show in which we traveled to and lived in six cities over one year, asking people what success really means to them. We lived out of hotels and Airbnbs, often unsure how we'd fund the next leg of the trip.

By the end of that year, we were over a million dollars in debt. The bank had taken my land. Our car had been repossessed. We sold furniture just to keep moving forward.

Eventually, we finished the project, and it went on to win multiple Emmy Awards. Standing on that stage, holding that trophy, I thought about all the nights we wondered if it was worth it. It reminded me that some of your proudest moments will only come if you're willing to push through the moments that make you want to quit.

YOUR PERSONAL BRAND MATTERS

If you're leading a company and not building your personal brand, you're leaving opportunities on the table every single day. Rather than buying from companies, people buy from people they like, trust, and know. The connection they feel with you often matters more than the product or service itself.

So, remember that your story is your greatest asset, and the worst thing you can do is keep it to yourself. Share it… All of it. Not only should you tell people about the big wins to prove what's possible. They also need to hear about the losses that taught you lessons you could never have learned in a classroom. In other words, share the moments that got you to where you are today, whether good or bad. The authentic behind-the-scenes moments just show you're human! Every piece of that story builds trust and credibility in a way no ad campaign can match.

I've landed some of my biggest opportunities because someone watched a single video I put out years earlier. They saw the journey, they saw the work, and they felt like they already knew me. That's the power of a personal brand. It's working for you 24/7. A perfect example of this happened to me on LinkedIn. I posted a simple update about a project I was working on. It was nothing flashy, just an authentic glimpse into what was happening in my world.

A few days later, someone I had never met commented and then sent me a direct message. They'd been following my content for months without ever saying a word. That single post was the spark that led to a conversation, and within weeks, I was in a room with investors and entrepreneurs I might never have met otherwise. It wasn't the post alone that made it happen, though. It was the trust built over time by consistently showing up and sharing my story.

The more people understand the real you, the more they'll want to work with you, invest in you, and bring you into rooms you didn't even know existed. That's more than marketing, it's leadership!

LEADERSHIP CAN BE LONELY

One thing people don't talk about enough is how lonely entrepreneurship can be. I've felt it at every stage. When I was starting out with no team, hauling Arctic Sticks in the back of my truck, and wondering if anyone believed in the vision. Now, I feel it as the Co-CEO of BIG Brand Ventures with dozens of people counting on me. The pressure never disappears. In some ways, it only gets heavier.

When you're the one with the vision, responsible for the mission and playing a big role in the future for your team and your clients, there are days when it feels like no one truly sees the weight you're carrying.

I've had moments in hotel rooms, right after speaking on big stages, where I sat alone and thought, "Does anyone really understand what this takes?" I've felt it after winning an Emmy and still waking up the next day with the same challenges staring me in the face. Even after launching a documentary, scaling companies, and working with people I grew up watching on TV, I've had days where the doubt crept in, and I wondered if I could keep pushing forward.

That's when I remind myself that we can't do it alone. You need people who get it, understand the grind, have the long nights, financial risk, and the emotional toll. I've been lucky to have mentors, partners, and friends who could meet me in those moments, who could say, "Yeah, I've been there, too," and mean it.

Leadership will always have its lonely stretches, but that doesn't mean you have to lead alone. Surround yourself with people who understand your world and believe in your vision. That's what keeps you moving when the weight feels too heavy to carry by yourself.

FROM BRAND TO LEGACY

Everything I've built started the same way: by putting myself out there, telling my story, and taking consistent action long before anyone was paying attention. When I was driving hours to pitch Arctic Stick to gas stations, or filming episodes for *Ambitious Adventures* with barely enough budget to cover the crew, I wasn't thinking about legacy. I was thinking about making the next right move. But looking back, those moments were laying the foundation for everything that followed.

Your brand is so much more than a logo, tagline, or polished website. It's the reputation you build by showing up. Not just when things are going well, but when they're falling apart behind the scenes. It's how you treat people when the cameras are off and the consistency of your values when deals fall through, projects flop, or you're fighting to make payroll. Those moments matter as much, if not more, than your highlight reel. Over time, that's what shapes your legacy.

When you build something rooted in authenticity, you create opportunities you could never predict. I've had speaking gigs, partnerships, and investments come my way from people who had been quietly following my journey for years. They saw the work, they saw the persistence, and they trusted me enough to open doors I didn't even know existed.

Don't get me wrong, you'll never feel "ready." I didn't feel ready when I cold-called my first potential investor. Or when I walked onto a stage with thousands of people in the audience. I didn't even feel ready when I co-founded a company with one of my childhood business heroes. But I showed up anyway.

That's what building a personal brand is all about. Show up when it's uncomfortable and take massive action. Your brand is your leadership and impact. When multiplied over time, your impact becomes the legacy you leave behind.

BRANDON T. ADAMS

Brandon T. Adams is the Co-CEO and Co-Founder of BIG Brand Ventures with Kevin Harrington, which is a Marketing, Advisory, and Investment Firm that scales product-based companies. He is also a 2X Emmy Award-Winning Producer, TV Host, Podcaster, and one of the producers behind the film *Think and Grow Rich: The Legacy*, which is the movie based on the book *Think and Grow Rich* written by Napoleon Hill. His video marketing strategies over the past 10 years with his portfolio companies have resulted in over $100 Million raised through a combination of revenue, crowdfunding, crypto, and equity fundraising. His sole focus today is scaling the products in the Big Brand Ventures portfolio and working towards bringing BBV to a billion-dollar brand.

www.BrandonTAdams.com

LEGACY OF LOVE

BY ANALEE VIZCARRA VINYARD

AUTHOR OF "A LEGACY OF LOVE," SPEAKER, CHRISTIAN LIFE COACH, INTERPRETER, & TRANSLATOR

Arranged marriage is a type of union in which the bride and groom are selected by individuals other than the couple themselves, particularly by family members, usually the parents or, as in my case, by my grandparents.

In our culture, arranged marriages happen. As you might imagine, it's not exactly a topic that's easy to bring up with family. I wondered: Who knew what? And when? But there were clues. When I was fifteen, not long after my mother, Alma, had died and we'd gone to live with my grandparents, I overheard one of my aunts arguing with them. She scolded my grandfather, "You hurt Alma!" I didn't understand what she meant at the time. I wouldn't for many years.

It was only recently, looking back on my story, that this same aunt filled me in. "What happened to you," she said, "is because you are just like your mother, compliant and good-natured. Your grandparents took advantage of you. Your mother wouldn't stand up for what she really wanted. You wouldn't stand up for yourself either."

My mother never talked about the origin of her marriage to my father. That's not strange, though, as she was a very private person. She had mentioned how my grandparents were very controlling when she was younger, but I had no idea they'd forced her to marry my father.

I've since pieced my mother's story together. Mom's brother, Carlos, had introduced her to Jorge. They grew to really care for one another. Jorge was the boy she chose. "I think they would have gotten married," my aunt said. "But your grandparents objected." From this point, the story became hauntingly familiar. "They forbid her from seeing Jorge and insisted instead that she start talking to a boy they chose for her, a neighbor of theirs, Fausto."

My grandfather told her that while Jorge offered her no future as an amateur boxer, Fausto had a real future as a butcher. "With his salary, he will be able to provide nicely for a family." And that, it seems, was my grandfather's sole motivation: money.

I was sick to my stomach hearing this.

"Why do you think your grandparents wanted to take care of you and your brother?" she asked. "They wanted money from your mother's estate. They wanted child support from Fausto. This is the family shame."

Learning the truth only compounded my pain. I'd eventually found my way out of that shadow: I'd found the man of my dreams. Mom never did. These revelations were emotionally overwhelming. The sadness, depression, frustration, hopelessness, confusion, and outright anger I'd felt rushed back and multiplied—this time for what they'd done to my mother.

They took away her friend, her love, her hopes, her dreams for a life with Jorge. They imposed their own will. They robbed her of her full potential. This is among my deepest struggles: Every time I remember my mother, I'm brokenhearted to realize she carried a deep burden she never told me about.

I understand why she couldn't tell me, because I lived with the painful secret, too. She had to have felt the same confusion, betrayal, grief, and anger, but somehow she'd forgiven them. Her heart wasn't vengeful. She continued to honor and respect her parents.

You've heard the old expression, "If life hands you lemons..." Mom made lemonade.

Her arranged marriage began similarly to my own: she was falling in love with Jorge, while my grandparents began forcing her to talk to Fausto. They married in 1972, and I was born in 1973.

They started to have problems right away. She didn't want to be home with him. She ultimately learned to live with the situation, and I think she even developed caring feelings toward Fausto... but it wasn't enough. It wasn't love.

I remember this emotion very well from my own experience. The reality sets in; you're married. You can try... or you can be even more miserable.

My arrival changed things for Mom, as would my brother Jesse's later. Now she had children to consider. Her mission was to provide as safe and happy a home as she could for us. But I know there were times she'd think of Jorge. Those moments when I'd catch her staring off into the distance, I'm sure, she longed for what might have been.

My parents separated when I was two, and divorced when I was four. My only recollection of their being apart was at Christmas: my father brought me home a yellow and red dress from J.C. Penney.

They remarried, and Mom became pregnant with Jesse. My dad's schedule at the meat market started at 3 AM. My mother would rise early to send him off with a homemade lunch. Jesse and I would wait for him at the doorstep. He always brought home the best cuts of meat. My mother showcased her culinary skills, cooking carne asada, stews, tacos, and all the traditional Mexican favorites.

Those after-work hours are really the only happy times I remember with my father. He'd take us to the swimming pool. He would carry us up and down the stairs. He'd put us on his shoulders and play with us. We'd come home to an amazing supper. I vaguely remember piggyback rides to bed and goodnight kisses. Sadly, these are the only good memories I have of him—and they all occurred before I was seven.

Knowing what I know now, I realize my grandparents were perpetuating a generational curse. They'd done this to my mother, and then to me.

I met Jose at school. He started walking me to my classes. He was really nice. When my grandmother found out, she told me I would have to stop.

"This boy is not for you," she'd say. "There is a boy in Mexico for you, Bonifacio."

I wasn't interested in Bonifacio. I was very interested in Jose. My grandparents didn't care.

Jose invited me to the prom. Of course, I said yes, but I didn't have a dress. I told my Aunt Martha. She offered to make me a beautiful red lace dress with a black bow. Prom was amazing! We spent an unforgettable night singing, dancing, and taking pictures.

For me, it meant the joy of being able to fully enjoy the moment. No one knew about my life at home. No one saw my bruises, either the physical ones or the emotional ones. No one knew the exhausting manipulation or the deep confusion homelife brought me. For once, I was just a normal teenager with a boy who liked me. Although I didn't want the night to end, Jose got me home on time. On the way, he promised:

"You deserve to be treated like a princess."

I felt alive again for the first time since Mom's passing. Someone accepted me, cared about me, and protected me.

At home, my life was filled with emotional abuse. With Jose, I found respite. We talked between classes, growing to know each other deeply. Two weeks after Prom, Jose said he wanted to speak to my grandfather. He hoped for their blessing for us to continue dating. I wasn't sure his visit was such a good idea. I suppose I was hopeful at the time, thinking perhaps they would hear him out. After all, if they really loved me, why wouldn't they want me to be happy? It couldn't have gone worse.

Jose sat down with them and began telling my grandparents about his feelings for me and how our friendship was deepening and becoming more. He was open and honest about how we were taking a proper approach to our relationship, and he was hoping for their blessing for us to continue dating. He explained to them that his plan was to complete his university studies at Utah State and for me to complete my studies as well, so that we might later get married.

Grandpa was ruthless. "Married?! You have nothing to offer my granddaughter! She is beautiful, and you are not handsome! She is smart, and you are stupid!" Shocked by my grandfather's words and sickened at the way he had belittled Jose, immense sadness flooded my heart. I watched as Jose stood up, said good-bye, and walked out. He was humiliated.

The next time I saw him at school, everything was different. He was angry with me, as if I'd said those horrible things to him. I felt for him. He was deeply hurt and offended, and rightly so. He was a young man starting his climb into adulthood, trying to do the right thing, and my grandfather had broken his spirit.

Not long after, my grandparents informed me I would be marrying Bonifacio in Mexico. They announced these plans for me as I walked in the door from school. "We are taking you to pick out your wedding dress," Grandma said. I'd barely set my schoolbooks down before they whisked me out the door. Grandfather drove us to Bakersfield.

On the ride, my mind went back to the happiness of getting my prom dress a few months earlier. Getting my wedding dress was an occasion I'd always dreamed of. I'd always anticipated it would be one of the most memorable moments of my life. It was certainly going to be that… just not in the way or for the reasons I'd imagined. I was so confused. How could people who pledged to care for me force me into marriage?

We stepped into the bridal store.

"Who is getting married?" the salesperson asked excitedly.

"Our granddaughter is," Grandma replied. I couldn't protest.

"You pick out a dress," she said.

Each dress I tried on only deepened my depression. I so wanted to wake up and discover this had all been a bad dream.

I broke down crying in the dressing room. I longed for Mom to walk through the door and say, "Don't worry, mi hija! I'm here." I longed for Jose to swoop in and save me. I longed for someone, anyone, to come to my rescue.

Sensing I was taking too long, my grandfather sent Grandma back to see what was holding me up.

The strangest thing is, my grandparents expected me to be happy. They thought I should be excited to look at wedding dresses and look forward to my wedding ceremony. They couldn't understand my confusion and sadness.

But there would be no argument. "It will be the best thing for you," Grandma said. "We'll take you back to Mexico to marry Bonifacio."

I was furious. As my mother lay dying, my grandparents had promised to care for me—and this was their idea of care?

When the time came to travel to Mexico for the wedding, we drove for many, many hours. The entire way, I was hoping for someone or something, anyone or anything, to intervene and stop this wedding.

Once we arrived, I told a cousin of mine, "I don't want to do this."

She answered, "You need to talk to your grandparents again. Surely, they will understand you."

I resolved to try once more with my grandmother, this time as we were on our way to the hairdresser's to get my hair done for the wedding. "Please help me, Grandma," I pleaded. "If Mom were still here, she would not allow this to happen!"

This time, she shut me down hard, not even offering the familiar "talk to your grandfather" option, but rather emphatically stating, "We are already here! You will be married!

So much of who I am today is because of my mother. I give thanks for her—I was truly fortunate to have an amazing, loving example of a mother.

I suffered through an arranged marriage and lost my chance to have a first love of my choosing. I realized, as she had, the pressures of being in a loveless relationship and fighting to make it work for my children.

I'd go on to experience the tragic loss of a child—in her case, a forced abortion, and in mine, the malpractice of a doctor. Oh, but the good I inherited from my mom is a treasure! I inherited Mom's love for those who are hurting and in need. Her compassion. Her empathy. Her desire to meet others with kindness and encouragement.

Today, I'm thrilled to partner with several local charities and organizations, using my life, my story, and my recovery to benefit and even bless others. I've been able to share my story as a bridge for people who have been through similar heartaches and hardships, using my passion to help them recognize and embrace their true identity as a child of God, and to encourage them to turn their experiences into opportunities to embolden and bless others.

56

ANALEE VIZCARRA VINYARD

Analee Vizcarra Vinyard is a Christian Life Coach, Medical Interpreter, and Translator based in Texas. Fluent in both English and Spanish, she utilizes her language skills to serve diverse communities and has provided instruction to executives and government officials. Analee is also deeply involved in charitable organizations focused on assisting women affected by abuse and human trafficking, aiming to help them find healing and empowerment through faith-based initiatives.

In June 2022, Analee published her memoir, *A Legacy of Love: Finding the Courage to Finally Speak Out*, which recounts her journey from a challenging childhood to finding strength and purpose through faith. The book has received positive reviews for its inspiring narrative of resilience and hope.

At the age of fifteen, Analee's life was marked by profound loss and upheaval. Following her mother's death, she faced manipulation, control, and abuse, leading to a loveless arranged marriage at eighteen. Despite these hardships, Analee's unwavering faith in Jesus Christ guided her toward healing and a renewed sense of purpose.

Analee continues to empower others through her coaching practice, *My Dream LLC*, where she helps clients navigate various life challenges and achieve personal growth. She also contributes to her community by volunteering with organizations dedicated to supporting marginalized women. She currently has a cooking TV show with NowMedia TV called *Cook and Conquer*.

Analee pursued a Language Degree and a Medical Interpreting Certification with MiTio (Medical Interpreting and Translating Institute Online) in 2020 and holds a Christian Coaching Certification.

Residing in Texas with her husband, Joel Wren Vinyard, Analee embraces a fulfilling life dedicated to faith, family, and community service.

For more information about Analee Vizcarra Vinyard and her work, please visit her official website:

www.AnaleeVinyard.com
YouTube: *www.youtube.com/@analeev4658*

THE UNSHAKABLE LOVE THAT TRANSFORMS US ALL

BY DR. CONSTANTINE I. NIGHTINGDALE

VETERAN, COMMUNITY LEADER, INTERNATIONAL CHURCH LEADER, & ACCLAIMED AUTHOR

My name is Constantine Ikaika Nightingdale. I was born and raised in Hawai'i, a land rich in culture, resilience, and spiritual connection. Over the course of my life, I have worn many titles: veteran, executive chef, nonprofit CEO, international senior pastor, and bestselling author. At the core of it all, I am a servant of the Most High—a servant of humanity, of faith, and of a mission greater than myself: to lead with love and build bridges between people, communities, and nations.

I did not always know this path would unfold before me. Looking back, every moment, every hardship, and every victory was a stepping stone that prepared me to become the leader I am today.

THE POWER OF PURPOSE

Leadership, to me, begins with purpose. True leadership is not about accolades or visibility. It is about impact, rooted in service, guided by agape love, mercy, and grace.

As a U.S. Navy veteran, I learned the value of discipline, sacrifice, and honor. But it was my return to civilian life where I discovered a deeper calling, not just to serve out of duty, but to lead through compassion, listening, and action. I began by helping homeless veterans and Hawai'i's less fortunate, launching job-training programs and advocating for infrastructure improvements, such as bus routes, to support underserved communities.

Each initiative was more than a project. It was an opportunity to restore dignity and hope. Leadership is often about identifying a gap and choosing to be the one who fills it, even when it is hard.

BUILDING COMMUNITIES, LOCALLY & GLOBALLY

Leadership is not confined to one island, one city, or one pulpit. Over the years, I have led efforts across Hawai'i, supporting incarcerated families, underserved youth, kūpuna (elders), and those caught in the grip of gangs, prostitution, and exploitation.

As founder and CEO of three nonprofit organizations—Hawai'i Christian Dream Service Center, Hawai'i Christian Community Land Trust, and Hawai'i Christian Community Foundation—my mission has always been clear: to provide practical solutions that support spiritual, emotional, and economic growth.

This work eventually expanded globally. From the Philippines to Pakistan, Dubai to Africa, I have helped develop home churches, schools, prayer centers, and outreach programs. The goal has never been to push an agenda. It has always been to help people discover their purpose, rise from adversity, and lead with integrity.

WRITING WITH IMPACT

I never set out to be a bestselling author. But when I surrendered to the calling to write, the words flowed, not from me alone, but through divine inspiration. Sixteen books later, my writings have reached readers across continents, been featured at global book fairs, and sold in Target, Walmart, Barnes & Noble, Amazon, and major bookstores worldwide.

My stories explore faith, leadership, resilience, and prophecy, not to preach, but to invite readers into deeper reflection and discovery. Storytelling is one of the most powerful tools we have. It connects us, heals us, and helps us lead with empathy, understanding, and love.

THE SPIRIT OF IMPACT LEADERSHIP

No matter your background, faith, or profession, leadership starts with courage. The courage to step into your purpose. The courage to speak the truth, even when it is unpopular. The courage to keep going when the road is long.

Here is what I have learned:

- **Serve Before You Shine:** True leadership starts in the quiet moments, when no one is watching, and you are doing the right thing anyway.

- **Do Not Fear Failure:** I have had businesses close and ministries tested. Every setback refined me into a humbler and more strategic leader.

- **Lift Others as You Rise:** Whether through job training, outreach, or storytelling, your influence is a tool to help others rise.

- **Stay Grounded in Truth & Love:** In a world filled with noise and division, leaders who endure are those who lead with compassion, clarity, and purpose.

In a world that moves faster than ever, where opinions are loud, divisions are deep, and love often feels conditional, it is easy to wonder where we belong. But through all of life's noise and pain, I have come to understand one unwavering truth: there is a love so deep, so real, it transcends human limitation.

I have felt it, not through status, wealth, or praise, but in quiet moments of reflection, surrender, and connection with God. This love is not reserved for the perfect, the religious, or the righteous. It is for all of us. It is for you.

My journey began on the islands of Hawai'i, where I was born into a richly diverse heritage: Hawaiian, Portuguese, Hungarian, Chinese, German, Irish, Spanish, and Nigerian. We call it a "mixed plate." Just as my lineage has been a blend of joy, heartbreak, success, failure, searching, and finding, so has my life.

But the most powerful moment of my life was not external. It was internal. It was when I encountered unconditional agape love, the kind that asks for nothing but offers everything. For me, that connection came through my faith in Jesus. Beyond religion or doctrine, I discovered a universal truth: love is the foundation of everything good and lasting.

You do not need to be perfect to be loved. You do not need to have all the answers, follow every rule, or avoid mistakes. Love meets you exactly where you are and invites you into something deeper.

HOW TO ACCESS THIS LOVE

Whether you are spiritual, religious, or simply curious, there are practical ways to open your heart to something bigger than yourself:

- **Quiet Your Mind & Listen:** In today's world, silence is rare, but it is in stillness where we hear whispers of love, guidance, and truth. Read something that nourishes your soul. Reflect. Journal. Meditate. Listen for the voice within.

- **Pay Attention to the People Around You:** Sometimes the most divine messages come from everyday interactions: a friend's advice, a child's laughter, a stranger's kindness.

- **Notice Patterns in Your Life:** Life teaches us what we are ready to learn. Setbacks, challenges, and discomfort can guide us toward growth. Love does not always feel like comfort; sometimes it comes as truth.
- **Stay Open to Growth:** Whether you believe in the Trinity, universal energy, or the power of the human spirit, growth begins with humility. When we stay open, we stay teachable.

As someone who once believed I could not live without the love and guidance I found, I now say with full conviction: I will not live one second disconnected from it. Not because I am afraid, but because I have experienced the richness of what is possible when life is grounded in true agape love.

You do not need to subscribe to a specific belief to know that real love is transformative. It heals. It unites. It uplifts. It clarifies. And it never fails.

A FOUNDATION BUILT ON LOVE & TRUTH

There is a story that has stood the test of time, not just because of its history, but because of the transformation it brings. This story, told over the centuries through 66 books and more than 40 authors, is known as the Bible. It spans more than fifteen hundred years yet carries one unifying message: you are deeply loved.

One of its most well-known verses, John 14:6, says: *"I am the way, and the truth, and the life. No one comes to the Father except through Me."*

This is not a verse meant to exclude, but to invite. It is a call to understand a love so deep that it was willing to lay everything down for us. The life and sacrifice of Jesus Christ is a radical message of unconditional love, grace, and redemption.

AWAKENING THE HUMAN CONSCIENCE

Each of us is born with an internal compass, a voice that nudges us toward right and wrong, love and fear, peace and conflict. Some call it the conscience. Others call it divine guidance or soul wisdom. Regardless of belief, we all carry this inner voice, and how we nurture it determines the life we live and the legacy we leave.

At times, our conscience may be aligned, clouded, hardened, or even broken. I have experienced each of these states. Yet in every stage, agape love has met me with grace, healing, and restoration.

The more we pay attention, the louder that inner voice becomes, and the more we are able to walk in alignment with our values, our purpose, and our calling.

LEADING WITH AGAPE LOVE

True leadership begins not with power, but with presence. It is the awareness that we are part of something greater than ourselves. The most powerful leadership begins from within, rooted in truth, integrity, and divine love.

Agape love is leadership. It is love that listens, forgives, leads, and seeks direction from God or the inner spirit. Leadership is not about being the loudest voice in the room. It is about showing up, giving, listening, healing, and loving.

Your story, no matter how humble, painful, or unfinished, is the very tool someone else is waiting for. When you lead from your story, with integrity and faith, you give others permission to rise.

I am just one pebble on the beach. Through faith, agape love, and service, I have watched ripples become waves. And so can you.

Walk boldly. Lead humbly. Love relentlessly.

Your life is the message. Make it count.

With Aloha from Hawai'i,

Constantine Ikaika Nightingdale

DR. CONSTANTINE I. NIGHTINGDALE

Dr. Constantine I. Nightingdale is a prominent Christian author and preacher based in Hawaii, known for his fervent dedication to spreading the message of Jesus Christ. He identifies as the "End-Times" Apostle and focuses on preparing believers for the challenges of the modern world through his writings and sermons.

As the Senior Pastor of his church, Constantine leads a global congregation and emphasizes the importance of understanding and navigating contemporary spiritual challenges. He has authored several impactful books, including:

- **"Mormonism Debunked: A Former Mormon Discusses the Doctrines of Christianity vs. the Tenets of the Mormon Faith"**: In this work, Constantine draws upon his personal experiences to contrast Christian doctrines with those of the Mormon faith.

- **"The End Game: Survival Handbook for the End Times"**: This publication addresses current global issues from a Christian perspective, offering guidance on preparing for challenging times.

- **"How to Effectively Share Jesus with an Atheist: Or Someone Trapped in a Cult"**: This book provides strategies for articulating the gospel to individuals from diverse belief systems.

Constantine actively engages with various media platforms to disseminate his message. He has appeared on radio shows, including an interview with Benji Cole of CBS Radio, discussing his ministry and publications.

Despite his significant contributions, Constantine maintains a humble perspective on his personal biography, stating, "My biography is not important. But I praise and glorify the One who sent me—Jesus Christ."

Through his ministry and writings, Constantine continues to impact lives, guiding individuals in their spiritual journeys and understanding of contemporary faith challenges.

For more information on Dr. Constantine I. Nightingdale's work and teachings, you can visit his profiles on various platforms:

www.amazon.com/stores/author/B0BSNVCBYK
Facebook: *facebook.com/constantine.nightingdale*

PURPOSE, DIRECTION, & MOTIVATION: BATTLE-TESTED LEADERSHIP FOR A LIFE OF IMPACT

BY CRISTINA SOLIS WILSON

DECORATED COMMAND SERGEANT MAJOR, AWARD-WINNING AUTHOR, INTERNATIONAL SPEAKER, & LEADERSHIP STRATEGIST

THE CALL TO SERVE

Before I ever wore the uniform, leadership was already written into my DNA—I just didn't know how far it would take me.

Growing up in South Texas as the only girl among eight brothers, I learned how to speak up, stand firm, and hold my own. As a proud Latina, my identity shaped everything: my faith, resilience, work ethic, and unwavering loyalty to family. I watched my mother lead from behind the scenes with quiet strength and selfless grace. I knew I wanted to lead, too—but not just behind the curtain. I wanted to lead from the front, where real impact begins.

In high school and college, I found my spark in JROTC. I felt powerful in uniform. As a drill team commander and battalion leader,

I began to experience the true pulse of leadership. At that time, I thought leadership was about presence, performance, and getting results. But I would come to learn it was so much more than that. Leadership—real leadership—is about responsibility. It's about people. It's about service and why you serve.

I was the first in my family to attend college and the only girl among my siblings. When the time came to sign my ROTC contract, fear crept in. My father had served in the Air Force, so military life wasn't completely foreign—but as a Latina woman, it felt like I was stepping into uncharted territory. This wasn't just about a career choice; this was about breaking generational and cultural expectations.

I was scared—not because I lacked confidence, but because I lacked a roadmap. No one in my family had walked this path. But that's when my husband, Michael, became my anchor. He reminded me that leadership isn't about fitting into someone else's box—it's about answering your own call. With his belief in me, I found the courage to break the mold and take the leap.

I entered the military with passion, purpose, and a heart to serve—but I still didn't fully grasp what leadership would demand of me. It would challenge every part of who I was. It would stretch me in ways I couldn't imagine. And ultimately, it would transform me.

What I came to understand is this: leadership isn't about being in charge. It's about being accountable—to your mission, to the people you're entrusted to lead, and to your own values. Leadership, at its core, is not a position—it's a posture.

And that's what being an Impact Leader is truly about.

I joined the Army at twenty-nine—older than most—and boot camp wasted no time stripping away illusions. One inspection, in particular, changed me forever.

A younger female soldier in my platoon broke down under the drill sergeant's relentless pressure. It wasn't the task that broke her—it was the weight of emotional fatigue. She quit shortly after. That day, something clicked for me: the true battle wasn't physical—it was mental. The Army doesn't just train your body; it reconditions your mind. They're not looking for the strongest or the fastest. They're looking for those who can weather the storm, rise under pressure, and lead others through the fire.

What I didn't know then was how deeply that transformation would shape every part of my life.

The military breaks you down, not to diminish you—but to reveal the resilience, adaptability, and fortitude that's been inside you all along. It's in that breaking that you begin to rebuild—stronger, clearer, and more rooted in who you're meant to be. I came in with my own fire, my own grit, and my own sense of purpose—but the Army gave me the framework to turn those raw traits into refined leadership.

I fully embraced the Army's core values: Loyalty, Duty, Respect, Selfless Service, Honor, Integrity, and Personal Courage. Together, those values spell one powerful word—**LEADERSHIP**. And for me, that wasn't just an acronym. It was a roadmap.

But even more than that, I began to live by three guiding principles that would define my leadership: **Purpose. Direction. Motivation.**

Those three words became my compass—on the battlefield and in life.

This was the beginning of my transformation. What I once thought of as simply a career became a calling. And while I didn't realize it yet, I was being shaped into something far greater than I had imagined—not just a leader in uniform, but a leader who could inspire change beyond the ranks.

As I rose through the military, eventually becoming a Command Sergeant Major, I learned that true leadership wasn't just about commanding—it was about connecting. It was about being the calm in the chaos, the strength in the storm, and the steady voice when everything else was uncertain.

Leadership, I discovered, wasn't a chapter in my story.
It *was* my story.

And now, it's the story I share to help others rise because that's what impact leaders do. We don't lead for status. We lead for service. We lead for legacy. We lead because the next generation is watching, and the world needs more voices who lead with heart.

INTO THE FIRE

Leadership is not learned in theory—it is forged in fire. For me, that fire came in the form of combat zones, high-stakes decisions, and the sobering weight of knowing that lives depended on my clarity, courage, and character.

I didn't just study leadership—I lived it. I was tested in real time, in unfamiliar terrain, under pressure that demanded not perfection, but presence. Leadership wasn't an idea. It was a responsibility.

One of the most defining moments of my military career came during my deployment to Iraq. I was chosen to be a Convoy Commander—the only female selected for that role in our company at the time.

The others who held that title were experienced infantrymen—prior active-duty, combat-tested, and all ranked E-7 (Sergeant First Class). I was an E-6 (Staff Sergeant). I had no infantry background, and at that time, women weren't even allowed in infantry roles. On paper, I didn't qualify.

But leadership isn't defined by résumés—it's revealed in moments.

Those men—my peers and superiors—saw something in me. They recognized my instincts, my commitment, and the respect I had earned through consistent service. They didn't just train me. They advocated for me.

Their belief lit something in me that I'll never forget.

Yes, I was proud to become the first female convoy commander in our company. But what meant more was the realization that leadership has no gender. It has no limits. Leadership is about presence. It's about being trusted with the mission—and with people's lives.

Of course, impostor syndrome showed up. I questioned if I truly belonged. But I didn't let it stop me. I anchored myself in the same three principles that had guided me from the beginning:

Purpose. Direction. Motivation.

Before every mission, I started by asking the end-state question: *What outcome do we need to achieve?* Then, I would reverse-engineer every detail to align with that goal.

But I didn't stop at strategy—I brought my soldiers into the mission. *I explained the why.* I helped them understand not just what we were doing, but what they were part of. When people understand their **purpose**, they show up with more intention. When they have **direction**, they move with confidence. And when they feel **motivated**, they push past limits—not because they're told to, but because they believe in the mission.

That mindset created unity, loyalty, and fierce accountability.

I never had to demand trust. I earned it.

By leading with clarity.

By listening with respect.

And by showing up with conviction, even when fear was whispering in the background.

Leadership isn't about being the loudest voice in the room.

It's about being the calm in the chaos.

The anchor in the uncertainty.

The one who moves forward anyway—because others are depending on you to lead them there.

THE MOMENT THAT CHANGED EVERYTHING

Leadership isn't just about courage—it's about consequence. One decision can shift everything. And sometimes, the hardest lessons are the ones that make us the strongest leaders.

One day, while leading a return convoy from Camp Anaconda to Camp Cedar II, I made a call that tested every part of me. We were traveling along the MSR—our main supply route—when I believed we had missed our exit. I was in the lead truck, responsible for every vehicle and life behind me. With urgency rising, I gave my driver a direct order: "Take the next exit."

He hesitated. I could feel the uncertainty. But I was the convoy commander. I gave the command.

We took the exit.

The moment we veered off, I knew something was wrong. We had entered a dark, unsecured part of Baghdad. The road was narrow, flanked with concertina wire, and dim figures with weapons stood in the shadows. I couldn't tell if they were allies—or threats.

My heart raced—but my training was louder than my fear.

In seconds, I radioed the convoy. I ordered the rest of the trucks to stay on the MSR. The middle truck was instructed to take the lead, while those who had exited with me were guided back to the main route. I moved my truck to the rear, taking responsibility and covering the last vehicle as we reconnected.

We all made it back safely. But just days before, that same stretch of road had been lit up with small arms fire. The memory of that terrain wasn't just recent—it was raw.

That night changed me.

Not because I was proud of my decision—but because I had made a mistake. And I survived it.

I learned something that every impact leader must embrace: panic cannot be your pilot. Pressure cannot make your decisions.

Only calm and clarity can.

From that day forward, I committed to slowing down—just enough to think with presence, not panic. I learned to trust my team more deeply. I learned that even in leadership, humility is a strength, not a weakness.

That moment didn't define me because I failed. It defined me because I grew.

GROWTH BEYOND THE RANK

As I moved up in my career, so did my leadership evolution. I wasn't afraid to admit what I didn't know in the early years. I asked questions, sought out mentors, and stayed curious. My authority didn't come from my rank—it came from my relationships.

I earned trust by listening. I led by example—not by title alone.

I kept a notebook, wrote down everything I was learning, and treated each encounter with my soldiers as an opportunity to build trust, not demand it. That posture—of humility, learning, and service—became the foundation of everything I would do next.

Leadership is never about knowing it all. It's about showing up willing to grow, to listen, and to lead others with **Purpose, Direction,** and **Motivation**—not just for the mission, but for the people who trust you to carry it out.

THE TRANSFORMATION: FINDING YOUR WHY

Leadership didn't end when I took off the uniform.

In many ways, that's when it truly began.

The battlefield had given me powerful tools—discipline, resilience, and tactical clarity. But stepping beyond the military, I realized that leadership could evolve into something even more impactful. Service wasn't just a chapter in my life. It became the lens through which I saw the world—and my next mission.

Everything I had learned in the Army—about responsibility, decision-making, and leading with conviction—wasn't meant to stay confined to a base or a battlefield. It was meant to be carried into the spaces where people struggled to find purpose, direction, and hope.

So I began serving again—this time in my church, nonprofits, and the local community—and something clicked.

My leadership didn't need rank. It needed heart.

My mission didn't need a title. It needed alignment.

The same values that guided me through combat—loyalty, service, integrity, and courage—could transform lives in everyday settings.

That's when I understood: I was no longer just a military leader. I had become a *mission-driven* leader.

I didn't want to simply guide people—I wanted to equip them. I didn't want to command—I wanted to empower. And above all, I wanted to help others find their "why."

Because leadership, at its highest level, is never about control. It's about calling.

It's about showing others what's possible and helping them unlock the greatness inside themselves.

Today, my mission is to lead by example—to serve with purpose, to speak with clarity, and to remind people that their past does not define them, but their *why* will.

Purpose. Direction. Motivation.

These words didn't just shape my time in uniform—they became my philosophy for life.

People often told me, "You need to write a book. Your stories, your mindset—it's different."

While I haven't written a full memoir (yet), one message kept rising to the surface every time I spoke, mentored, or trained leaders: *Purpose. Direction. Motivation.* It was no longer just a military mantra. It had evolved into a life strategy, a mindset shift, and a guiding framework that could change lives.

That's why I wrote *Finding Your Why.*

The inspiration didn't come from wanting to be an author—it came from service. Years of mentoring and coaching revealed something to me: people were hungry for clarity. They were searching for identity, meaning, and significance—but didn't know where to start.

So, I built them a path.

In the book, I define your why as the intersection of your skills, experiences, passions, and values. Your why isn't just your job or your passion—it's the soul of your leadership. And it deserves to be discovered with intention.

I found my own *why* when I noticed a pattern: people consistently came to me for guidance, clarity, and connection. Whether I was leading troops in uniform or coaching entrepreneurs and women navigating leadership, I felt the deepest sense of alignment when helping others rise. That became my mission: to activate purpose in others.

And when that alignment clicked, everything changed.

I stopped chasing success and started creating *significance.*

One of the women I coached came to me discouraged, underpaid, and unseen in her workplace. As we worked together, she confronted the limiting beliefs that kept her playing small. She stepped into her why, reclaimed her worth, and eventually surpassed every peer in pay and position. That's what happens when purpose and power align.

And that is why I lead.

Because real leadership isn't about power. It's about *permission*— helping others give themselves permission to rise.

For me, it always comes back to what the Army taught me from day one:

Leadership is about influencing people by providing purpose, direction, and motivation.

That's not just something I teach. It's something I live.

And now, I pass it on—to you.

You are not here by accident. You're here to make an impact.

Find your why. And then, help others find theirs.

That's what being an Impact Leader truly means.

Lead with Purpose. Move with Direction. Stay Motivated.

My time in the military taught me this core truth: leadership exists to accomplish the mission and improve the organization. That framework never left me—it simply evolved.

Today, it shows up in how I serve my community, run my nonprofit, coach my clients, and speak to the next generation of leaders. The principles are timeless:

- **Purpose** is the *why* behind every action. It's what fuels me to keep showing up—even when no one's watching.

- **Direction** brings *clarity*. It ensures I'm not just busy, but impactful. Without it, I drift. With it, I lead.

- **Motivation** is the *fire* that sustains me, especially when things get tough. It's not about hype—it's about having vision, discipline, and a reason to keep moving forward.

This simple framework has become my compass. Whether I'm mentoring a young woman struggling to find her voice or standing on stage teaching leadership to hundreds, I always return to these three words, because they still work. And more importantly, they still *transform*.

Here's what I want you to know:

Leadership isn't about commanding—it's about *connecting*. It's not about rank or recognition. It's about becoming a person of influence because you live your values, not because you demand authority. Because you're grounded in purpose, aligned in direction, and committed to leading with heart and integrity.

You don't need a title to lead. You don't need permission to start making an impact.

You simply need to know who *you* are and why you're here.

Because when you know your why:

• You speak with clarity.

• You decide with confidence.

• You lead with presence.

That's why I wrote *Finding* Your Why. It's more than a book—it's a guide to uncovering the purpose already inside you and the courage to lead from it.

"The journey to finding our why is the most rewarding self-care you will ever give yourself."
~ Cristina Solis Wilson, Finding Your Why

You don't have to wear a uniform to lead with courage. You simply have to show up with **Purpose**, **Direction**, and **Motivation**, and trust that your impact will follow.

Because real leadership doesn't start on a battlefield—it starts *within*.

LEGACY IN MOTION

Leadership doesn't end when the mission is over—it echoes. It lives on through the people we empower, the values we pass down, and the confidence we help others discover in themselves. Titles fade. Uniforms come off. But *impact endures*.

For me, legacy isn't about being remembered for what I accomplished in uniform—it's about how I continue to serve beyond it. Yes, I'm proud to be known as a Combat Veteran. But even more than that, I want to be remembered as someone who helped others rise. Someone who turned challenges into change. Someone who led with Purpose, Direction, and Motivation—and taught others to do the same.

Every program I create, every keynote I deliver, every young person I mentor—I do it with one mission in mind: to activate others to lead from within. I want people to stop waiting for permission and start claiming the leadership they already carry inside.

Because here's the truth: the world doesn't need more followers—it needs *more impact leaders.*

One of the greatest reminders of that came through a young boy I met when he was just five years old in our local Cub Scouts program. My husband and I took him under our wing, mentoring him through hands-on activities that built not just skills—but character. Years later, he still calls us. Still seeks guidance. Still lets us walk beside him. Today, he's a focused and driven young chef with a passion for pastries—and a sense of purpose. Watching his transformation has been one of the most meaningful experiences of my life because that's leadership. Not just showing the way—but walking with someone long enough for them to realize they can lead too.

And then there are the moments that bring it all full circle—like when a woman I mentored once told me:

"I attribute my newfound confidence, my new life, and my ability to leave the military on a positive note to you. I will forever be grateful. Thank you for lifting me up."

That's why I share my story. That's why I lead.

Not to be seen, but so others can *see themselves.*

So, here's my invitation to you:

Don't wait for the perfect title, the perfect time, or the perfect version of yourself. Leadership doesn't wait for permission. It begins right where you are.

You already have the tools. You have a voice. You have a mission.

You have a story that someone else needs to hear.

Start here:

What is your *purpose?*

What is your *direction?*

And what fuels your *motivation?*

You may not have all the answers today—but the moment you start asking, your leadership journey begins.

And when you lead from within, you don't just change your life.

You change the lives of everyone around you.

Let your legacy be a life of *Purpose. Direction. Motivation.*

If you've connected with this chapter, I invite you to reach out— whether for a podcast, a panel, or a powerful conversation on stage. I'm here to bring purpose-driven leadership into more rooms, more communities, and more hearts. Because leadership isn't about one voice—it's about lifting *many.*

More than anything, I hope you turn this page feeling **empowered**, **confident**, and **clear**.

Because you matter.

Your voice matters.

And your leadership journey *matters*.

If my younger self could see me now—the girl who once wondered if there was space for someone like her to lead—she'd smile and say: *You did it. I'm proud of you for rising above the noise and answering the call.*

Now it's your turn.

Your legacy starts here.

And it starts now.

— **Cristina Solis Wilson**

CRISTINA SOLIS WILSON

Cristina Solis Wilson is a distinguished Combat Veteran with over 26 years of exemplary service in the U.S. Army. A decorated military professional, she has completed six deployments and earned numerous accolades for her commitment to discipline and courage. Cristina holds a Bachelor of Science degree in Criminal Justice from the University of Texas-Pan American, complemented by over two decades of law enforcement experience.

As Chief Strategy Officer at Entrepreneur Power Network, Cristina's dynamic leadership style draws upon her military experiences, making her a highly sought-after keynote speaker, leadership strategist, and mentor. Her journey reflects resilience, continuous improvement, and a profound commitment to service.

In addition to her military contributions, Cristina is a dedicated entrepreneur and CEO of CM Institute of Leadership, LLC. Here, she empowers the workforce through coaching, training, and leadership speaking engagements. In 2012, she co-founded

Crossroads Academy, a non-profit aimed at cultivating leadership skills among economically disadvantaged youth.

Cristina is also an International Trainer and Coach for the John Maxwell Team, contributing significantly to the *"Transformación Paraguay"* project, which trained over 20,000 Paraguayan leaders.

Cristina's commitment to leadership education is reflected in her service with the Hispanic Women's Network of Texas-RGV Chapter (HWNT-RGV), where she led the organization to be recognized as the 2023 Chapter of the Year under her leadership. She is also the co-founder of AMVETS Post 107, which was established in 2017 to support and uplift local veterans and their families.

Cristina's influence extends beyond professional achievements. A Yale School of Management Women's Leadership Program graduate, she continues to elevate her impact through lifelong learning. She has been recognized as the *2025 Author of the Year* by the International Impact Book Award, the *2025 Inspirational Influencer Trailblazer Award* recipient by the International Association of Women, the 2025 *Business Woman of the Year* by the RGV Hispanic Chamber of Commerce, the 2024 *Latina of Influence* by Hispanic Lifestyle, and the 2023 *Women of Influence* by SUCCESS Magazine. Her accolades also include the *Estrella de Tejas* Award (2022), *Hispanic Women Making History* Award (2022), and *Women of Distinction* Award (2017).

In 2022, she and her husband, Michael, were also honored with the Network Lead Exchange *President's Award*, a national recognition presented at the NLX Conference for their outstanding contributions to the growth and success of their company.

Actively engaged in her community, she supports organizations such as the RGV Hispanic Chamber of Commerce, HWNT, the Organization of Women Executives (OWE), and the National Hispanic Professional Organization (NHPO). She balances her professional pursuits with her role as a devoted wife to Michael and a nurturing mother to Michelle and Christian.

As the award-winning author of *Finding Your Why*, which won the International Impact Book Award in 2024, Cristina offers invaluable insights that inspire others to unlock their potential. She is a force for positive change, leaving an enduring mark on all she influences. She embodies the philosophy of embracing adversity for continuous improvement.

www.CrisWilson.com
LinkedIn: *www.linkedin.com/in/Cristina-Solis-Wilson*

THE POWER OF ROOTED LEADERSHIP: GROWING INTO YOUR FULL POTENTIAL

BY ERICA GIFFORD MILLS

FOUNDER OF BALANCED SYMMETREE &
INTERNATIONAL WOMEN SPEAKERS SUMMIT, AWARD-
WINNING AUTHOR, INTERNATIONAL SPEAKER,
EMPOWERMENT COACH, & TALK RADIO HOST

Leadership is not merely a position to be assumed or a title to be held; it is a way of being. It is the capacity to influence, inspire, and transform both us and those around us. Rooted leadership is about standing firm in our core values while remaining flexible in our approach, embracing growth even when the path is uncertain, and leading with purpose while empowering others to rise alongside us.

In this chapter, we explore the principles of rooted leadership, from mastering self-leadership and breaking limiting beliefs to building emotional intelligence, cultivating resilience, and leaving a legacy that honors our unique stories. Each section interweaves both timeless strategies and deeply personal experiences that illuminate what it truly means to grow into your full potential.

ROOTED IN SELF-LEADERSHIP:
MASTERING THE INNER GAME

Great leaders are rarely defined by external accolades or the titles they hold. Rather, they are marked by their internal mastery and the quiet strength that comes from knowing who they are at their core. Before we can truly lead others, we must first lead ourselves, with clarity, discipline, and unwavering confidence.

THE JOURNEY OF SELF-LEADERSHIP

Self-leadership begins with cultivating self-awareness, a practice that involves honest introspection into our strengths, weaknesses, emotions, and motivations. I have experienced many adversities in my life that have forced me to confront the deepest parts of my soul. I witnessed the unexpected death of my father, an event that shook the very foundations of my being, all while I was grappling with my own challenges. Shortly after, my mother's failing health through cancer and dementia/Alzheimer's further underscored the fragile nature of life. These experiences taught me that true leadership begins by first understanding and leading oneself through pain and uncertainty.

BUILDING A FOUNDATION AMIDST ADVERSITY

When our personal world is rocked by tragedy, it is easy to feel unmoored. I have faced a stroke at 42, aggressive breast cancer at 49, and, perhaps the most shattering, the loss of my only child at 51. Each of these challenges brought its own set of trials. From enduring 20 rounds of chemotherapy, multiple surgeries including a double mastectomy, countless blood infusions, and fluid treatments, to the emotional toll of grief and loss. Yet, in these darkest moments, I discovered a strength that lay hidden beneath fear. I learned that leadership, especially self-leadership, is forged in the crucible of adversity.

It is in these moments that we truly come to understand that our worth is not measured by our outward appearance or achievements, but by our resilience and our capacity to rise after every fall.

REFLECTION: CULTIVATING YOUR INNER STRENGTH

Consider the moments when life challenged you most. How did those experiences shape your inner dialogue? Reflect on your strengths and vulnerabilities. By acknowledging the pain and learning from it, you lay the foundation for a leadership that is both compassionate and resilient. Each trial, whether the unexpected death of a loved one or the physical toll of battling disease, can become a stepping stone toward a deeper understanding of who you are and the leader you are destined to become.

THE POWER OF MINDSET:
BREAKING LIMITING BELIEFS

One of the most formidable obstacles on the path to leadership is the invisible barrier of limiting beliefs. These are the mental chains that can imprison us long before we ever step into a leadership role. Thoughts like "I'm not ready," "I don't have enough experience," or "What if I fail?" can stifle our potential and diminish our ability to lead effectively.

REWRITING THE NARRATIVE THROUGH ADVERSITY

For me, one of the most challenging aspects of mindset was cultivating self-love and acceptance during my battle with breast cancer and the overwhelming grief of losing my son. The scars, the hair loss, and the physical toll all challenged my confidence and sense of identity. But leadership demands that we rewrite our narratives. I had to remind myself that strength is not in appearance, but in resilience. That beauty is not in perfection, but in perseverance. That worth is not measured by what I have lost, but by the courage I have shown in the face of overwhelming pain.

TRANSFORMING LIMITING BELIEFS

A rooted leader acknowledges these limiting beliefs but refuses to be defined by them. Instead of succumbing to fear, they harness it as a catalyst for growth. Consider this transformation:

- **Limiting Belief:** "I don't have enough experience to lead."
- **Empowering Belief:** "I am constantly learning and evolving. Every experience, even those steeped in pain, adds to my leadership capacity."

When we shift our mindset, every setback becomes a lesson and every scar a testament to our journey. Regularly challenging our inner narratives and replacing limiting beliefs with empowering ones allows us to reclaim our power.

REFLECTION EXERCISE:
TRANSFORM YOUR INNER NARRATIVE

Take a moment to write down a limiting belief that has held you back. Next, consider one painful experience, perhaps a moment when you felt vulnerable or broken, and transform that memory into an empowering narrative. This exercise is not just about replacing words; it's about healing the wounds of the past and setting a course for a future defined by resilience and strength.

EMOTIONAL INTELLIGENCE:
THE SECRET TO INFLUENCE

In the realm of leadership, knowledge and strategy are essential, but the most powerful tool a leader possesses is emotional intelligence (EQ). This skill set transcends technical know-how, tapping into empathy, self-awareness, and social skills that are vital for building lasting relationships and fostering a supportive environment.

The Five Pillars of Emotional Intelligence

- **Self-Awareness:** Recognizing and understanding our emotions is the cornerstone of effective leadership. Amid personal loss and physical suffering, I learned that acknowledging every emotion—no matter how painful—is crucial to healing and growth.

- **Self-Regulation:** Managing emotions constructively, especially during crises, is key. My battles with illness and grief required me to find ways to channel fear and sorrow into determination.

- **Motivation:** Purpose-driven leaders persevere through setbacks. My journey, marred by unimaginable hardships, fueled a motivation to advocate for causes close to my heart.

- **Empathy:** Understanding the perspectives of others, particularly during times of loss, builds a foundation of trust and support. Empathy allowed me to connect deeply with those who were also facing adversity.

- **Social Skills:** Effective communication and conflict resolution are essential. As I navigated personal tragedies, I learned to communicate my vulnerabilities, inspiring others to share their own stories.

ENHANCING EQ THROUGH PERSONAL TRIALS

My experiences with a stroke, cancer, and the death of my beloved son taught me that emotional intelligence is not merely a tool for professional success—it is a lifeline in times of personal crisis. By embracing vulnerability and learning to navigate my emotions, I developed a leadership style that is authentic and deeply compassionate.

Exercises for Cultivating Emotional Intelligence

- **Active Listening:** Practice being fully present in conversations, especially when discussing difficult topics. This nurtures deeper connections and trust.

- **Mindfulness:** Engage in mindfulness practices to remain aware of your emotional state. These practices can be especially grounding during turbulent times.

- **Feedback:** Invite honest feedback from trusted friends or mentors. Their insights can provide clarity and guide your emotional growth.

- **Empathy Building:** Reflect on your own hardships and consider how they might resonate with others. This reflection can enhance your ability to connect on a profound level.

CULTIVATING RESILIENCE: THRIVING THROUGH CHALLENGES

No leadership journey is without setbacks. Every leader, no matter how accomplished, faces moments of adversity. What sets truly great leaders apart is not the absence of challenges but their ability to bounce back, learn, and emerge stronger. Resilience is the capacity to thrive in the face of obstacles, transforming failures into steppingstones toward success.

EMBRACING LIFE'S STORMS

I have encountered profound personal tragedies, as identified earlier, from my parents' death, stroke, to breast cancer, to the heart-wrenching loss of my only child. When I thought I was returning to normal, life turned upside down, and my world was shattered once again. My son was my pride and joy, my sunshine; his passing, especially under the unbearable circumstances of his own decision to end his battle with inner demons, left me in deep shock and grief.

These experiences taught me that resilience is born from the very act of surviving hardship. Every moment of despair was a call to stand up again, to fight harder, and to honor the memory of those we have lost by living boldly.

STRATEGIES FOR STRENGTHENING RESILIENCE

Here are several practical strategies to help you build resilience:

- **Reframe Challenges:** See setbacks as lessons in disguise. Each failure, each painful memory, holds the potential for growth.

- **Build a Support System:** Surround yourself with mentors, peers, and advisors who understand your journey and can offer guidance in your darkest hours.

- **Practice Self-Care:** In the midst of chaos, remember to care for your physical, mental, and emotional well-being. Your survival depends on it.

- **Celebrate Small Victories:** Recognize every step forward, no matter how small, as proof of your strength and determination.

A PERSONAL BLUEPRINT FOR RESILIENCE

Reflect on the adversities that have shaped you. Write down the lessons learned from each challenge, whether it was the intense physical battles with illness or the deep emotional scars left by personal loss. Use these reflections as a blueprint for future challenges, reminding yourself that even in the most broken moments, you possess an inner strength that is both profound and transformative.

ROOTED IN VISION: LEADING WITH PURPOSE

A leader without vision is like a tree without roots, easily swayed and lacking the enduring impact that comes from a deep sense of purpose. Vision is the anchor that keeps us aligned with our values and the compass that directs our decisions. It's the force that propels us forward, even when the road ahead is shrouded in darkness.

CRAFTING A VISION AMIDST PERSONAL TRIALS

In the midst of my own journey through loss and illness, I was forced to confront profound questions about purpose and legacy. I realized that my struggles were not in vain; they were the impetus for a vision that went beyond personal survival. I became passionate about advocating for enhanced mental health awareness and treatment for active military personnel and veterans, honoring the memory of my son, who lost his battle with inner turmoil.

I also dedicated myself to empowering women navigating their breast cancer journeys with humor and dignity, reminding them that even the most aggressive battles can be fought with grace and resilience. My vision, forged in the fires of personal pain, is a beacon for those who feel lost in the darkness.

Exercises to Clarify Your Vision

- **Vision Board:** Create a visual representation of your aspirations, including images, quotes, and symbols that represent not only your personal growth but also the causes you are passionate about.

- **Personal Manifesto:** Write a manifesto that outlines your core values, leadership goals, and the legacy you wish to leave behind. Let this document be a testament to your journey, a guide for your

- **Goal Mapping:** Break down your vision into actionable, measurable goals. Celebrate each milestone as proof that even in the face of unimaginable adversity, progress is possible.

TAKING BOLD ACTION: THE COURAGE TO LEAD

Vision without action remains a dream. To lead effectively, one must step into discomfort, make difficult decisions, and view failures as steppingstones to success. Bold action is the manifestation of a courageous spirit, a spirit that dares to challenge the status quo, even when life's challenges seem insurmountable.

STEPPING BEYOND FEAR

My personal narrative is punctuated by moments when the weight of adversity nearly compelled me to give up. The physical and emotional toll was immense. And then, when I lost my only child, a loss that left my heart shattered, I found myself teetering on the edge of surrender. Yet, every time I considered giving up, I remembered that true leadership lies in the courage to take even the smallest step forward. The decision to speak up in a meeting, to propose a new initiative, or to simply share my story with others, all these acts, though small in isolation, accumulated into a legacy of bravery and resilience.

CONFRONTING THE PARALYSIS OF LOSS & PAIN

Overcoming the paralysis induced by grief and fear was not an easy task. I had to learn that my scars were not symbols of weakness but emblems of survival. I had to understand that the beauty of my journey was found in my perseverance, not in a flawless appearance.

By acknowledging my vulnerability and sharing my story, I not only reclaimed my power but also paved the way for others to confront their own adversities with courage and authenticity.

ACTION CHALLENGE:
EMBRACE YOUR NEXT BOLD STEP

Identify one bold leadership move that you have hesitated to take. Whether it's advocating for a topic of great personal interest, setting firm personal boundaries, or sharing your personal journey to inspire others, commit to that action this week. Document your experience and reflect on how facing your fears transforms not only your leadership but also your entire perspective on life.

ADAPTING TO CHANGE:
THE KEY TO SUSTAINABLE LEADERSHIP

In a world defined by constant flux, change is inevitable. Effective leadership requires adaptability, the ability to pivot in response to new challenges without losing sight of your core values. Rooted leadership means remaining grounded while dynamically adjusting your strategies to meet the evolving demands of your environment.

NAVIGATING LIFE'S SHIFTS

My journey has been punctuated by unexpected turns and the unthinkable moments when I was forced to redefine my sense of normalcy. Each of these moments taught me that while change can be painful, it also opens the door to reinvention. Embracing change is about acknowledging the inevitability of life's uncertainties and using them as opportunities to innovate, grow, and redefine what is possible.

Practical Steps for Leading Through Change

- **Stay Informed:** Continuously educate yourself and stay aware of trends and shifts in both your personal and professional spheres.

- **Communicate Transparently:** Open dialogue about change fosters trust. Share your vision and the rationale behind your decisions, even when they are driven by personal necessity.

- **Encourage a Growth Mindset:** Cultivate resilience within your team by modeling adaptability and emphasizing that change is an opportunity for transformation.

- **Flexibility in Execution:** Be willing to adjust your strategies as circumstances evolve, ensuring that your core values remain intact even as your methods shift.

ROOTED IN SERVICE: EMPOWERING OTHERS

True leadership transcends personal gain. At its core, leadership is about service: uplifting others, recognizing their unique potential, and creating an environment where everyone can flourish.

The legacy I now strive to build is one of service and advocacy: for enhanced mental health support for our active-military personnel and veterans, for women navigating the tumultuous journey of breast cancer with humor and dignity, and for anyone seeking to set authentic boundaries and embrace vulnerability.

SERVING THROUGH PERSONAL EXPERIENCE

I know firsthand the transformative power of service. I have seen the darkness that grief can cast, but I have also witnessed how sharing your story can light the way for others. By advocating for myself and others, I have learned that service is not just an act of giving; it is an act of healing.

THE POWER OF ENCOURAGEMENT & MENTORSHIP

Empowering others begins with active listening, recognizing the unique strengths of those around you, and providing them with the opportunities to grow. Whether it's mentoring someone who is struggling with their own challenges or simply offering a word of encouragement, each act of service creates a ripple effect that transforms communities.

BUILDING A CULTURE OF TRUST & GRATITUDE

As a leader, I have come to understand that gratitude is one of the most powerful tools at our disposal. Expressing gratitude for every small victory, especially in the face of relentless challenges, reinforces a culture of mutual respect and resilience.

Let your leadership be defined by a commitment to lift others, to stand in solidarity with those facing their own battles, and to create a legacy that honors the struggles and triumphs of life.

THE LEADERSHIP LEGACY:
LEAVING AN IMPACT THAT LASTS

Leadership is not confined to a single moment or achievement; it is a lifelong journey of continuous learning, adaptation, and evolution. The legacy you leave behind is the cumulative result of your actions, decisions, and the lives you touch along the way.

REFLECTING ON A JOURNEY DEFINED BY RESILIENCE

Every trial, be it the heart-wrenching loss of a parent, the grueling health battle, or the profound sorrow of losing a child, has contributed to the tapestry of my leadership journey. These experiences, as painful as they have been, have imbued me with a unique perspective on life and leadership. They have taught me that the true measure of a leader is not found in external accolades but in the ability to transform personal tragedy into a beacon of hope for others.

CREATING A LEGACY OF ADVOCACY & EMPOWERMENT

The legacy I am striving to build goes beyond personal survival—it is about advocacy and empowerment. It is about encouraging authentic boundary setting and vulnerability so that every individual can reclaim their narrative, no matter how many adversities they face. This is a legacy born from pain but defined by perseverance and compassion.

YOUR CALL TO ACTION: STEP INTO LEADERSHIP TODAY

Leadership is a continuous journey of self-discovery and growth. I invite you to take immediate, actionable steps toward becoming the leader you were meant to be. Reflect on these guiding prompts:

- **Identify One Leadership Strength You Will Amplify:** Embrace the qualities that have carried you through your own trials and let them shine as a beacon for others.

- **Recognize One Area for Growth & Develop a Strategy for Improvement:** Embrace your imperfections as opportunities for learning and transformation.

- **Empower Someone Else by Offering Mentorship, Guidance, or Advocacy:** Use your experiences, both the scars and the triumphs, to inspire and uplift those around you.

Your leadership is not just about your personal journey; it is about the lasting impact you create in the lives of others. Stand firm in your values, share your story with authenticity, and let your resilience be a guiding light for those navigating their own storms.

PUTTING IT ALL TOGETHER: THE BLUEPRINT FOR ROOTED LEADERSHIP

Embrace Self-Leadership: Begin with an honest exploration of your inner self. Recognize how the adversities you have faced have shaped your inner strength.

1. **Transform Your Mindset:** Rewrite the narrative of your life. Replace limiting beliefs with empowering ones by recognizing that your scars are symbols of survival and your journey, no matter how painful, is a testament to your resilience.

2. **Develop Emotional Intelligence:** Nurture your capacity for empathy, self-awareness, and effective communication. Use your experiences to connect deeply with others who are navigating their own challenges.

3. **Cultivate Resilience:** Transform every setback into a lesson. Use your personal blueprint to empower yourself and others to rise stronger after every fall.

4. **Craft & Share Your Vision:** Let your vision be informed by your experiences. Advocate for causes close to your heart. Share this vision with passion, creating a roadmap for change.

5. **Take Bold, Courageous Action:** Step beyond the fear of failure. Every act of courage reinforces your leadership.

6. **Adapt & Innovate:** Embrace change as an opportunity to grow. Remain flexible in your strategies while staying true to the core values that have carried you through life's hardest moments.

7. **Serve & Empower Others:** True leadership is measured by the impact you have on others. Use your story to inspire those who feel overwhelmed by their own struggles.

8. **Build a Legacy:** Reflect on the lessons learned from every trial. Let your legacy be defined not by what you have lost, but by the strength you have shown, the causes you have championed, and the lives you have touched.

THE JOURNEY FORWARD: A PERSONAL INVITATION

As you finish this chapter, let it serve as both a roadmap and a rallying cry, a call to embrace every aspect of your journey, including the pain and loss, and transform it into a legacy of empowerment and hope. Remember, leadership is not about perfection; it's about perseverance, growth, and the courage to continue despite overwhelming odds.

Visualize yourself as a mighty tree with deep, resilient roots nourished by every experience, both joyous and painful. Even when the winds of change threaten to uproot you, your strength and authenticity will keep you grounded, while your branches reach out to inspire those around you.

Today, I invite you to take a deep breath, stand tall, and step boldly into your role as a leader. Embrace the journey of self-discovery, acknowledge the pain that has shaped you, and transform it into a source of strength for yourself and others. Your leadership is a gift, a beacon of hope in times of darkness, a legacy of resilience, advocacy, and transformative impact.

Are you ready to harness the power of rooted leadership? The world awaits your unique story and the inspiration you offer by turning personal adversity into a catalyst for positive change. Stand firm, lead with authenticity, and let your journey be the guiding light for others navigating their own storms.

Here's to rooted leadership: Inspire, empower, and transform!

ERICA GIFFORD MILLS

Erica Gifford Mills is an international speaker, award-winning author, and empowerment coach who helps women stop shrinking, stop asking for permission, and start leading with authority, confidence, and impact. She is the founder of Balanced Symmetree, a leadership and personal growth brand rooted in resilience, boundaries, and visibility, and the creator of the International Women Speakers Summit, a global platform dedicated to amplifying women's voices on and off the stage.

Known for her grounded presence and no-nonsense approach, Erica blends lived experience with leadership strategy to help women turn their stories into influence, without burnout, people-pleasing, or performative confidence. Her work centers on what she calls Rooted Leadership: leading from clarity, emotional intelligence, and aligned action rather than hustle or approval.

A breast cancer survivor and mental health and suicide prevention advocate, Erica's mission is deeply personal. After the loss of her only son, she chose to transform grief into purpose; creating spaces where women can speak honestly, lead boldly, and build legacies that matter. Her advocacy work supports military families, veterans, and community-based mental health initiatives, reinforcing her belief that leadership is not about perfection, but presence.

Erica has been recognized as a Top 10 Coach and has shared her message across stages, media platforms, and coaching programs internationally. Whether she is mentoring speakers, hosting powerful conversations, or challenging women to take up space, her message is clear: "Your voice is not optional, and visibility is a responsibility."

She doesn't teach women to be louder. She teaches them to be undeniable.

www.BalancedSymmetree.com
LinkedIn: *www.linkedin.com/in/EricaGiffordMills*

THE FIRE THAT FORGES A LEADER

BY BARON JAMES GRAY ROBINSON, ESQ

WORLD-RENOWNED AUTHOR, LAWYER, HEALER,
SPEAKER, COACH, MENTOR, & FILMMAKER

There are many misconceptions about how people become leaders. Many say leadership isn't born; it's forged in the fire of adversity. If that's true, my leadership journey began with an inferno—a raging burnout that consumed my identity, purpose, and desire to continue the path I had meticulously crafted for 27 years.

I was born into a legal dynasty. My grandfather was a judge in Eastern North Carolina during the Depression until he died in 1945. My father was a West Point graduate who ranked 3rd in his Duke University Law School class in 1953. He became a legend in North Carolina, notorious for his fierce style of litigating and broad expertise in all areas of the law.

I have three brothers, one a twin brother. He became a doctor; the others followed me into the law. I was born in 1953 to a predestined career path. My mother was the daughter of one of the wealthiest men in the South, my namesake, James Gray. My maternal grandfather was the chairman of the board of RJ Reynolds Tobacco Company. Both of my parents had high ambitions for their sons. My father's passion was practicing law and making money, and he was extremely successful at both.

I adored my parents. Unfortunately, they were "helicopter parents" and micromanaged my life down to the clothes I wore, the food I ate, and the people I associated with. They chose the college I would attend, Davidson College. I wasn't particularly interested in school or motivated by much at that point in life. I was more interested in living a bohemian life without the discipline my parents forced on me.

My college career was unimpressive, but I did have one bright spot on my record. I was the first president of my fraternity, Sigma Phi Epsilon, to become president in my junior year. Usually, the president was a senior; for some reason, my brothers saw something in me that they liked and elected me president.

During my freshman year of college, I encountered two profoundly life-changing experiences that shaped my understanding of existence. The first was my near-death experience after falling off a building. I landed on a brick wall, shattering all the ribs on the left side of my body and losing inches of skin from my face.

Yet, the physical trauma was overshadowed by a spiritual awakening —I found myself floating above my broken body, observing the frantic attempts to revive me. There was no fear, no pain, only a euphoric sense of peace and safety. I was enveloped by radiant lights that spoke to me, assuring me that I was "close" to death but had a purpose yet to fulfill. Those words anchored me back into my body, and I woke up in the college medical infirmary with a renewed sense of destiny.

The second transformative experience that year was learning Transcendental Meditation, which had been introduced to the U.S. in 1971 by Maharishi Mahesh Yogi. Astonishingly, the deep meditative state I achieved mirrored my near-death experience—an overwhelming sense of detachment from the physical, an expansion of consciousness, and a blissful connection to something greater than myself. These two events, though starkly different in origin, illuminated for me a singular truth: there is a vast, boundless reality beyond the limits of the physical world, and my purpose was to bridge it with my life's work.

When it became time to decide what to do after college, I still had no passions or ambitions. I thought being a behavioral therapist at Outward Bound would be worthwhile, but my parents made it clear that if I wanted to stay in their good graces, my only option was to go to law school. I didn't want to be a lawyer, but it had one great advantage: I could delay reality for three years while in law school.

Oddly enough, I nailed law school. I had remarkable grades, for a time, in the top ten in my class. I was an editor of the Law Review, a justice on the Moot Court Board, and the president of my legal fraternity, Phi Delta Phi. If anything, I should have recognized my leadership abilities—but honestly, I was simply doing what needed to be done to survive. My peers saw it before I did and elected me to leadership roles without me ever volunteering. It wasn't planned, it just happened.

I fulfilled my parents' dream when I joined my father's law firm out of law school. It was not a happy experience. It was clear that everyone felt I did not deserve to be there despite my law school record. Ironically, my father's nepotism put a bullseye on my back. After a few years, I had to admit to myself that the pressure the firm placed on me to prove myself and my general dislike of the practice of law led me to resign. I moved to another city and became the owner of a popular restaurant.

Long hours in the kitchen, balancing orders, and managing a restless staff taught me the weight of leadership faster than any handbook could. Two years in, exhaustion settled in and told me its hard truth —if I was going to pour that much of myself into something, it should be the law. So, I wiped down the counters one last time, handed over the keys, and moved back to my hometown.

As soon as I moved back home, I had another near-death experience. I had played rugby since college; it was just the right mixture of violence, skill, and camaraderie. During my (last) rugby game, an opposing player accidentally ran the top of his head into my face, crushing it flat. I again left my body and had an experience that was like the feelings I had when I fell off the college building. I experienced a sense of joy and euphoria; all my past sins were forgiven.

As they wheeled me into the operating room to repair my crushed face, through my haze, I heard the surgeon say: "Just remember, I can't make a silk purse out of a sow's ear." (Looking in the mirror today, I think he did a Grayt® job.) One of the transformative aspects of my near-death experiences was the realization that I was given a new chance to live. As they would say today, I was rebooted. It is an exhilarating and freeing experience!

I secured a position at a law firm owned by several classmates and advanced quickly through the ranks. I became a partner, then a managing partner. I did well because I led by example and worked harder than anyone else. I was well-liked and started making more money. I was still stressed, but at least I had something to show for my efforts. Then, one day, my father knocked on my door and offered me a position in his firm.

Again, to win my parents' praise and respect, I joined his firm against my better judgment. I quickly became a partner and started to enjoy the perks of hard work. I accepted leadership roles in community affairs and my church. I became chairman of the board of the local substance abuse facility; I served on charity boards, and I did everything I could to serve.

I was a third-generation trial attorney specializing in family law and civil litigation in North Carolina. The law was in my blood. It was my birthright, my legacy, and my future. From the outside, I had everything—success, respect, financial security—but inside, I was crumbling under relentless pressure. The constant battles in the courtroom, the emotional weight of my clients' lives, and the never-ending cycle of the stress of trying to live up to everyone else's expectations left me physically, mentally, and spiritually depleted.

In hindsight, I can see that things could have been different if I had the tools I have now to manage stress and turn challenges into fun in a challenging career.

In 2004, I did what many consider unthinkable: I walked away. I had no safety net, no plan, and extreme disapproval from my family, but none of that mattered. All that mattered was my undeniable need to escape the chaos before it consumed me completely.

I didn't realize then that stepping away wasn't the end of my journey. On the contrary, it began a transformation that would shape me into the leader I was always meant to be.

BREAKING DOWN TO BUILD BACK UP

Burnout wasn't just exhaustion but a complete disintegration of my identity. Without my law career, who was I? For the first time in my life, I had no title to lean on and no external validation to define my worth. I was forced to confront myself in the rawest, most vulnerable way.

Rather than falling into despair, I became obsessed with understanding what had happened to me. I delved into neuroscience, neurobiology, neuroplasticity, epigenetics, and mind-body-spirit medicine. I pursued over 30 certifications in law, healing, and coaching. I trained under some of the world's foremost experts in wellness, transformation, and resilience. I became the confidant and advisor to three internationally recognized spiritual leaders. It was an enlightening experience to observe how these individuals managed their thousands of followers. Some taught me how to be; others taught me how not to be. I took it all in, eager to heal myself and, in turn, help others avoid some of the self-created obstacles that had hindered me.

Little by little, I started piecing myself back together—not as the attorney I once was, but as someone who could help others navigate their own battles with stress, anxiety, addiction, depression, and burnout.

FROM SURVIVOR TO LEADER

As I healed, people began to seek me out: attorneys, professionals, entrepreneurs, executives, doctors, and parents facing the same struggles I once did. They saw in me a mirror of their own suffering, but more importantly, they saw hope. They saw someone who had walked through the fire and emerged stronger. Even those who didn't know of my near-death experiences told me that there was something different and unique about being around me.

Leadership wasn't something I sought out. It was something that found me. I wasn't trying to build a movement; I was trying to help people survive. But the more I shared, the more I realized my story wasn't just mine—it belonged to countless others who felt trapped in a life burning them alive.

This realization became the foundation of my mission: to turn stress into success, to transform breakdowns into breakthroughs, and to teach others that leadership isn't about titles—it's about impact.

THE MAKING OF A LEADER: KEY LESSONS

Through my journey, I learned a deep understanding of what true leadership looks like. Here are the most crucial lessons I learned:

1. Resilience & Adaptability: Reinventing Yourself When the Old You No Longer Serves

Leadership isn't about sticking to one path; it's about knowing when to pivot. I had to abandon the identity I spent decades building and embrace a new purpose. That kind of transformation requires resilience and a willingness to adapt. Every leader will face moments where the road ahead is unclear. The key is to trust that even in uncertainty, growth is happening. NEVER QUIT. I did not quit my life's purpose and mission when I stopped practicing law; I merely pivoted to my true path.

As I indicated, I didn't want to be a lawyer; I only wanted my parents' respect and love. I believe that a true leader will find their path eventually and recognize when they are trying to put a square peg in a round hole. Remember that all growth is uncomfortable, and when things get difficult, have faith and confidence that you will accomplish your goals.

2. Leadership is About Who You Are, Not What You Do

One of the misconceptions of success is that we must make everything happen. After all that I have experienced and learned, the truth is we manifest what we are, not what we desire. A leader takes responsibility for their team's success and "unsuccess." What we experience reflects who we are. When we don't like what we see in the mirror, we don't change the mirror.

We must examine our thoughts, emotions, and motivations to ensure they align with our vision. Teams look to the leader to see how to behave. If the leader is committed, transparent, supportive, and inspiring, their team will be, too. Anyone not following that example will stick out like a sore thumb. People relate to those who demonstrate that they care about their well-being. A large part of who you are as a leader involves vision, mission, and passion. I like to say that the leader has the vision and motivation and shares that with their group. Surround yourself with people who share a mission, vision, and passion.

3. When You are Leading by Example, Be Happy & Have Fun

We have all been in a meeting or gathering when the boss walks into the room. The mood (energy) depends on what the team has been doing, whether problems must be solved, and the group's success (or losses). Then, the boss walks into the room. People focus on the boss's facial expressions, body language, and demeanor. Before the boss says a word, the group will know whether the meeting will be positive or negative. People react accordingly to the tone the boss sets.

If the boss is relaxed, smiling, and confident, their staff reflects the same. If the boss is upset, the people will be upset, and the meeting will probably not go well. Some people call this vibrational energy. If the boss raises the room's vibration, things will go well. If the boss lowers the vibration, there will be problems. You can imagine which scenario will turn out for the best.

This same concept applies to the business, the office, the family, and the world. If you are positive and happy, your experience of the business, office, family, and the world will be far different than if you are negative and upset. The leader sets the tone and creates the team's "reality."

Neuroscience tells us that the autonomic nervous system determines your experience in life. This subconscious decision to be in your Warrior mode (sympathetic nervous system) or Guru mode (parasympathetic nervous system) changes your brain's thoughts and operations. You automatically enter Warrior mode when you are threatened, upset, worried, or confused. This interferes with your ability to problem solve.

When you are in Guru mode, you can relax, communicate, collaborate, and problem-solve. I teach people how to hack their brains to stay in Guru mode. Guru mode is how you are supposed to be, your default mode. If you are worried, upset, angry, or depressed, you have been in Warrior mode too long. Be happy and be a guru.

4. Be Humble & Support Your Team

No one becomes wealthy or stays wealthy on their own; it takes teamwork to acquire and keep true wealth. Successful leaders have the knack for surrounding themselves with people who are good at what they do. I am the first to acknowledge my team of about 20 people who make the mission happen. I could not serve the people on a global scale without them. When they do something well, I let them know it.

When I receive awards and accolades, I acknowledge them. I let them know they are doing a Grayt® job when I see them. We are hard-wired to form groups, for in the community, we find safety. Make your group your tribe. Give them a common purpose and support them in every way you can.

With all my philanthropy, I always gave credit to my parents. There are several plaques in the Manu Rain Forest Preserve in Peru with my parents' names on them for the water projects I funded. There are schools in India named after my parents. Recognizing others for their contributions to our success reminds us that it is a group effort.

5. Vision & Purpose-Driven Leadership: Leading with Impact, Not Ego

Before my burnout, my success was measured in wins, prestige, and financial gain. After my transformation, I realized leadership isn't about personal achievement—it's about impact. My mission shifted from personal success to helping others reclaim their lives. Leaders don't chase titles; they chase purpose.

Ironically, when this happens, the accolades will come. You don't have to be successful to be a leader. When I was in college and became the president of my fraternity, I probably had the worst GPA of the bunch. However, I wanted to make our fraternity a tribe, a family, and a refuge for those souls who were competing and trying to thrive. I suspect that my near-death experience instilled in me the values of resilience, empathy, and grace.

6. Empathy & Emotional Intelligence: The Superpower of Great Leaders

Having walked through my own crisis, I developed a deep empathy for those struggling. Emotional intelligence—understanding, listening, and connecting with people on a human level—is one of the most powerful tools a leader can have. People will follow those who genuinely care. Our brains are hardwired (1) to survive and (2) to connect with others. Both constructs are based on the feeling of safety.

In line with this key trait, know who you lead. Be transparent with them, and they will be transparent with you. Mistakes will be made, but if people are supported rather than criticized, they will be inspired to learn from their mistakes and improve. An ounce of support is worth a pound of criticism. It is never a mistake if you learn something.

7. Crisis Management & Problem-Solving: Thriving Under Pressure

As an attorney, I had to perform in high-stress environments. But it wasn't until I faced my own personal crisis that I truly understood leadership under pressure. Real leadership isn't about avoiding problems; it's about embracing challenges as opportunities for growth. Leaders have the ability or a plan to deal with the stress of challenges. I teach leaders how to do this; it isn't difficult once they know how. Leaders know that an ounce of support is worth a pound of criticism. While it is necessary to help your team understand the mission and the vision, letting them know they are valued and supported will empower them to achieve these goals.

One of the critical keys to leadership: not taking anything personally. Remember to stay in Guru mode, and everything will work out. Sometimes hard decisions must be made, but let the team have input into your decision-making process. Whenever possible, make it a group decision.

8. Mentorship & Influence: Leadership is About Who You Lift Up

I realized that my greatest impact wouldn't come from what I achieved but from what I helped others achieve. Whether mentoring attorneys, coaching executives, or guiding professionals through burnout, leadership empowers others to step into their own greatness. I don't think of myself as a leader; I think of myself as a teacher.

When I realized that "we" is more powerful than "I," I was able to reach more people. After all, "we"llness is much preferable to "i" llness.

THE GLOBAL IMPACT OF LEADERSHIP

The more I embraced my role as a leader, the greater the opportunities became. I began speaking internationally, training high-level executives, and consulting with businesses on leadership, resilience, and transformation. My work has been featured in the ABA Journal, Attorneys-at-Work, Family Law Journal, Holistic Life Magazine, The Wall Street Journal, GQ, and other top publications. I've authored 13 books, many of them award-winning and bestsellers, designed to help professionals thrive in high-stress environments.

Beyond writing and speaking, I dedicated my life to philanthropy. I funded clean water projects in the Amazon, orphanages in India, African schools and orphanages, and medical clinics worldwide. True leadership is about service; nothing has been more fulfilling than giving back to those in need.

MEDIA & STORYTELLING AS LEADERSHIP

Recently, I expanded my impact through Beyond Entertainment Global, LLC, a media production company dedicated to transformational storytelling. My documentaries, including Beyond Physical Matter, Beyond the Mastermind Secret, and Beyond Physical Life, will reach audiences worldwide, sharing messages of healing and empowerment. Beyond Physical Matter won best documentary at the 2024 Miami Film Festival.

It's ironic—after leaving the practice of law, I never imagined I'd find myself in front of a camera, sharing my story with millions. But leadership doesn't take you where you expect; it takes you where you're needed.

Leadership doesn't necessarily require dealing with people. Many leaders lead through their written word. I have written numerous books and articles; many are posted on my website, *www.jamesgrayrobinson.com*.

Explore the alchemy of leadership in my books:

How Big is Your But? (International Book Award and Amazon Bestseller)

What is Love? (International Book Award and Amazon Bestseller)

Dying to Live, Living to Die

Reflections Journal

The Secrets to Healing (International Book Award and Amazon International Bestseller)

A Guide to Preventing Burnout for Executives Thriving in the Legal Arena (Amazon)

A Comprehensive Guide to Wellness in Law (ABA)

The Guru and The Warrior (Indigo Press)

The Southern Book of the Dead

Compilation Books

The Change Vol. 20

Cracking the Rich Code Vol. 13

A LEGACY OF TRANSFORMATION

My work has been recognized globally. I was knighted by the Royal Order of Constantine the Great and Saint Helen, awarded the

President's Lifetime Achievement Award, and honored with the International Humanitarian Award. Yet these accolades pale in comparison to the real reward: the lives changed through my journey.

Every day, I hear from people who found hope in my story. People who were on the verge of giving up but found the strength to fight another day. That's what leadership is. It's not about perfection. It's about using your story to lift others up.

FINAL WORDS:
LEADERSHIP IS A CALLING, NOT A CHOICE

I would have laughed if you had told me 20 years ago that I'd be an international speaker, healer, and transformational leader. I was a trial attorney, trained to fight, argue, and win. But life had a different plan for me. Leadership isn't something you choose. It chooses you. It calls you through your challenges, your struggles, and your pain.

The question is: will you answer?

I did. And it changed everything.

And if there's one thing I know for sure—it's that something Grayt will happen to you today.

BARON JAMES GRAY ROBINSON, ESQ

Baron James Gray Robinson, Esq, is a distinguished healer, coach, author, speaker, and philanthropist, renowned for his unique integration of legal expertise and holistic wellness practices. With over 50 years of professional experience, he has dedicated his life to empowering individuals to transform stress into success.

Professional Background:

- **Founder & Attorney Coach at Awakened Mastery Inc.:** Established in 2020, Awakened Mastery Inc. focuses on assisting litigation attorneys, entrepreneurs, and professionals in managing stress, preventing burnout, and enhancing both personal and professional fulfillment.

- **Legal Career:** Before transitioning to coaching, Baron James held partnership positions at esteemed law firms, including Robinson & Lawing, LLC (1991–2004) and Hendrick, Zotian, Cocklereece & Robinson LLC (1984–1991). He began his legal career as an associate at Hudson, Petree, Stockton, Stockton, and Robinson

Educational Qualifications:

- **Juris Doctor:** Earned from Wake Forest University School of Law in 1978.

- **Bachelor of Arts in English: Graduated from Davidson College in 1975.**

Holistic Wellness & Coaching Expertise:

In response to personal experiences with stress and burnout, Baron James expanded his expertise by acquiring over 32 certifications in various disciplines, including law, healing, and coaching. His training encompasses neuroscience, neurobiology, neuroplasticity, epigenetics, and brain/heart integration.

Publications & Media Contributions:

- **Author:** Baron James has penned several books, including Thriving in the Legal Arena: The Ultimate Lawyer's Guide for Transforming Stress into Success, which won the 2024 International Lifetime Impact Award.

- **Filmmaker:** He produces documentaries promoting wellness and personal growth, with projects like "Beyond Physical Matter" highlighting the healing power of the mind.

Accolades:

- **Presidential Lifetime Achievement Award:** Recognized for his significant contributions to society.

- **International Humanitarian Award:** Scheduled to be presented in November 2025, acknowledging his global impact on wellness and healing.

Philanthropy & Community Engagement:

Beyond his professional endeavors, Baron James serves on the board of directors for the SQ Foundation and has contributed as a legal consultant for SQ Worldwide & SQ Foundation. His philanthropic efforts include speaking engagements and writings that inspire individuals to achieve a balanced, fulfilling life.

Personal Philosophy:

Drawing on his extensive experience, Baron James advocates embracing challenges as opportunities for growth and emphasizes the importance of integrating mind, body, and spirit for holistic well-being. His journey reflects a profound commitment to personal transformation and helping others navigate the complexities of modern life with resilience and purpose.

www.JamesGrayRobinson.com
LinkedIn: *www.linkedin.com/in/Gray-Robinson-*

MY JOURNEY TO ACHIEVE EDUCATION

BY KIMLY HOANG-NAKATA, M.ED.

DEVOTED MOTHER, WIFE, AWARD-WINNING AUTHOR &
EDUCATOR, MINDSMART SPECIALIST, GLOBAL KEYNOTE
SPEAKER & LEARNING SUCCESS COACH

A CHILDHOOD SHAPED BY NATURE & RESILIENCE

Before I learned to read or dream of a future beyond my village, I walked barefoot along the dirt roads of Central Vietnam, feeding the chickens at dawn and falling asleep to the sound of crickets at night. My childhood was deeply connected to nature, family traditions, and the challenges of post-war Vietnam.

Life in our rural village was simple yet demanding. I remember tracing shapes in the dust with a stick, imagining they were letters and symbols from a language I had yet to learn. We woke to the call of roosters, tended to daily chores, and played under the moonlight. On windy days, my brothers and I flew kites over vast rice fields. During flood season, we built rafts and picked fruit from floating trees. But woven into this beauty was the reality of hardship. Family was everything, and respect for elders and ancestors was a fundamental value instilled in us from a young age.

Those early rhythms shaped how I show up for others. Seasons taught me patience. Chores taught me shared responsibility. Respect taught me to hold space for many voices, not just the loudest ones. I did not have words for leadership then, yet I felt it in the way my grandmother divided tasks, in the way neighbors helped one another after storms, and in the quiet expectation that we would do our part. Leadership is not a title. It is a daily way of caring for the people in front of you, even when the work is ordinary, and the audience is small.

SEEDS WITHOUT SOIL: THE STRUGGLE FOR EDUCATION IN POST-WAR VIETNAM

My parents believed fiercely in the power of education. At six, I was filled with anticipation. My grandmother sewed me a book bag from an old raincoat, and I eagerly attended my first class. But that excitement faded the day I faced humiliation in front of my peers.

The spelling test was a nerve-wracking experience. I stood on a wooden chair behind a curtain while the teacher dictated words. My left-handed writing smudged across the board as my hands trembled. When the curtain was drawn, revealing my work, the classroom erupted in laughter. My heart pounded as I read each word aloud, my voice barely audible. That day, I walked home slowly, ashamed and defeated, knowing I would be punished again for using my left hand.

Despite the trauma, I refused to give up on learning.

That curtain moment became a promise I carry into every classroom. No child should be made small for the way their brain or body writes, speaks, or solves. I learned to repair the environment before I identified the learner.

When I plan a lesson today, I ask three simple questions that change outcomes. Can a student answer by speaking, drawing, or pointing? Can the first success be earned in the first two minutes? Can we celebrate effort so that courage grows while skill catches up? These questions help me lead with dignity and design learning that includes more children from the first minute.

A FAMILY'S DETERMINATION TO START ANEW

My parents were relentless in their desire to build a better life for us. My father, once a high-ranking officer in the Army of the Republic of Vietnam, lost everything after the Fall of Saigon in 1975. He endured years in a re-education camp, facing harsh treatment and limited opportunities. But he never lost hope.

Then, one evening, he heard a radio broadcast announcing the Humanitarian Operation (H.O.). Program, a rare opportunity for former South Vietnamese soldiers to immigrate to the United States. No one believed it was possible, but my father did. He traveled to Hue City every week, navigating the grueling application process with quiet determination. Against all odds, we were approved.

We became the eighth family in the Humanitarian Operation (H.O.) Program, embarking on a journey that would change our lives forever.

From my father, I learned two kinds of strength that rarely receive applause. Quiet paperwork courage, and patient hope. He stood in lines, filled forms, and returned the next week. He held a future in his heart long enough for the rest of us to see it. When I guide teams now, I remember that real change often looks like a checklist, a calendar reminder, and a promise you keep for months. It does not always look heroic, yet it moves families forward. That is leadership, too.

STARTING OVER IN AMERICA

Arriving in a new country was both thrilling and terrifying. We stepped off the plane into a world of unknowns, new language, unfamiliar customs, and cold winters that bit through our thin jackets.

I was placed in third grade by mistake, though I should have been in fourth. I could not speak English. Kids thought I was mute. I kept my head down, hiding in silence.

But one person saw beyond the silence, Mrs. Jones, my teacher. She introduced me to William, a kind boy who patiently taught me numbers while we played hopscotch at recess.

English still felt like a mountain I could not climb. So, I turned to books, and they became my safe place. I spent hours in the library, stacking children's picture books taller than myself at the checkout counter. One day, I stumbled across a bilingual book, and everything changed. For the first time, I fully understood a story in English. Not only the words, but the feeling, the rhythm, the meaning. In that moment, something shifted, and I not only learned English—I belonged.

That single bilingual book was my turning point. It was the bridge between two worlds.

Mrs. Jones and William showed me that small acts can change a life. A paired recess game. A bilingual story at the right moment. A teacher who says, "I see you." We can design belonging on purpose. A welcome in two languages at the door. A partner who teaches by playing. A librarian who walks a child to the shelf that will open a new world. These are simple decisions, yet they multiply courage in quiet hearts.

THE RELENTLESS PURSUIT OF KNOWLEDGE

I learned to shift my mindset from struggle to strategy. Like my father, I sought solutions instead of dwelling on obstacles. Education became my anchor. I committed to focused work each day, knowing I was paving a path not only for myself, but for my younger brothers. I translated school forms for my parents, helped my brothers with homework, and we tirelessly worked to rebuild our lives.

Fueled by purpose, I pursued my teaching credential and later earned a master's in education. My passion grew beyond textbooks. I immersed myself in neuroscience and wanted to understand how the brain learns. I learned that no two children process information the same way. Each one has a unique map to success.

This understanding led me to design personalized learning strategies. Alongside my husband, a pediatrician, we created the MindSmart Learning Program to help students develop thinking skills as a foundation for problem-solving, emotional regulation, and lifelong learning. Thinking builds independence and empowers students to adapt, grow, and thrive in a changing world.

I also began writing bilingual children's books, stories that serve as bridges across generations, cultures, and languages. I believe every child is unique and deserves to see themselves in a story and to feel seen in the world.

As MindSmart took shape, I learned that a vision needs structure to help real families. We wrote short routines that any classroom could run. We translated instructions so caregivers could try them at home. We created feedback cards that asked three questions: What helped this week? What felt hard? What should we try next? Turning big ideas into small habits made the work possible on a busy Tuesday, when most real change happens.

I began tracking a few simple measures our teams could use without a spreadsheet. Time to settle. Number of independent starts. Repairs after conflict. When those numbers moved, we celebrated and documented what we had done so others could replicate it. When the numbers did not move, we adjusted the plan and tried again. Progress became a shared story, not a private report.

I also learned to honor culture and language in practical ways. I practiced names until I could say them well. I invited family wisdom into meetings and read aloud in two languages whenever I could. Inclusion lives in details like that. It is a simple kind of leadership that keeps doors open for more children to walk through.

A MOMENT THAT CHANGED EVERYTHING

One of my most powerful teaching moments came with a student diagnosed with ADHD. He struggled to sit still and to focus. When I helped him understand how his brain worked, that his prefrontal cortex, Captain Cortex, could help him plan and stay calm, he began to take charge of his learning.

We added movement breaks, breathing exercises, and comic strip reflections. Slowly, he transformed. The child who once disrupted class began to lead study groups and mentor others.

That is the heart of MindSmart. We teach children how their brains work so they can build strategies and stop blaming themselves. When kids understand that their alarm system, Amy the Alarm, is sounding out of fear, they learn not to fear the feeling. They learn to listen, breathe, and move forward.

Helping him name Captain Cortex and Amy the Alarm changed more than his grades. It changed who he believed he could be in a room. He stopped introducing himself as a problem and started practicing leadership. He set a timer before tests, reminded peers to breathe, and showed a younger student how to draw a comic to process a hard day. Sometimes, leadership begins with a pencil sketch and a new word for an old feeling.

PARENTING WITH EMOTIONAL SAFETY

As a mother, I have seen how emotional safety begins at home. When my five-year-old son cried over a broken toy, I did not rush to fix it. I kneeled beside him and said, "You are really upset because your toy broke. That makes sense. I am here with you."

Then we breathed, stretched, and drew the moment into a comic strip. Together, we processed the feeling, rather than dismissing it.

Children do not learn to regulate alone. They co-regulate with us. Every time we name emotions, pause to breathe, and validate their experience, we teach resilience.

Home is the first leadership lab. I try to model what I hope my son will one day offer to others. A calm voice when traffic is slow. A real apology when I lose patience. A small routine that helps the nervous system settle. Children remember how we made the room feel. That memory becomes the script they use when they lead.

MODELING EMOTIONAL SKILLS AT HOME

Let us explore everyday habits that nurture emotional health:

- **Stay Calm During Stress:** Pause, breathe, and explain. "That traffic was frustrating, and I am staying calm." Children mirror this composure.

- **Talk Through Emotions:** Use stories and everyday language. "I am disappointed, and I will take a walk to feel better." It teaches emotional vocabulary.

- **Repair After Losing Control:** Apologize when you react harshly. It shows accountability and trust.

- **Prioritize Self-Care:** Explain your limits. "I need rest so I can be my best for you." It normalizes healthy boundaries.

- **Co-Regulate During Meltdowns:** Stay nearby and calm. Your nervous system becomes their anchor.

- **Build Regulation Routines:** Try deep breathing at bedtime, reading MindSmart Stories, stretching after school, or gratitude journaling. These rituals build resilience.

When families practice even one of these habits each day, we see shifts that last. A child who breathes before homework begins is more likely to start without resistance. A parent who repairs after a hard moment teaches accountability more clearly than any lecture. These moves are small and steady, and they shape culture at home and at school. Connection helps kids learn and grow.

In schools and homes alike, I have seen the transformation that emotional safety brings. Teachers who connect before correcting.

Parents who regulate themselves first. These moments build trust, and from trust, learning blossoms. Strong bonds don't just shape hearts—they shape minds.

Parental involvement is a cornerstone of children's educational success, influencing many aspects of their academic and social development. Research consistently shows that active engagement from parents leads to better educational outcomes, including higher grades, improved behavior, and stronger social skills.

When I meet with families, I begin with three questions. What are your child's strengths? What brings your child joy? What helps your child feel safe? Starting there turns a meeting into a partnership. We make better plans when we build with the people who know the child best.

WAYS PARENTS CAN POSITIVELY IMPACT THEIR CHILDREN'S EDUCATION

1. Encourage a Love for Reading

Reading with children from an early age fosters literacy skills, creativity, and cognitive development. Parents can make reading a daily habit with bedtime stories, library visits, and interactive reading activities.

Dr. Patricia A. Edwards developed the Parents as Partners in Reading program, which empowered parents to engage in effective book-reading practices. This initiative led to significant improvements in children's reading abilities and showed the lasting impact of parental involvement in literacy.

2. Establish a Structured Learning Environment

Consistent routines and a distraction-free space for studying at home can significantly enhance a child's ability to focus. A structured learning environment was at the core of the Catalyst project in Australia, where schools emphasized explicit instruction and disciplined learning spaces. Students saw measurable improvements in academic performance, which shows that structure plays a key role in a child's ability to retain information and focus.

3. Encourage Open Discussions About Learning

Regular conversations about school experiences help children process information and express concerns. This practice supports cognitive development, memory recall, and emotional intelligence.

4. Be Actively Involved in School Activities

Attend school events, engage with teachers, and participate in parent-teacher meetings to gain insight into a child's academic progress. Lynn McDonald's Families and Schools Together, or FAST, brings families into schools for weekly meetings to build protective factors around at-risk children. This involvement has been linked to increased student motivation and lower dropout rates.

5. Promote a Growth Mindset

Encourage children to view challenges as learning opportunities and to practice perseverance. Dr. Billy Hudson's story illustrates this. Despite a traumatic childhood, a teacher's belief in his potential changed his trajectory. He later earned a doctorate and founded Aspirnaut, a program that helps struggling students develop a growth mindset. This reinforces that intelligence and skills can grow with effort and support.

6. Implement Positive Parenting Practices

Adopt an authoritative style that balances warmth, support, and clear boundaries. This approach is associated with higher academic performance and better social skills.

Parents are leaders in every sense. A bedtime story is a leadership act because it builds attention and language. A study corner cleared of noise is a leadership act because it protects focus. A calm conversation after a hard day is a leadership act because it teaches regulation. What we model multiplies.

CHALLENGES & CONSIDERATIONS

While the benefits of parental involvement are clear, challenges such as financial constraints, language barriers, and limited time can hinder engagement. Educators and policymakers must recognize these obstacles and create inclusive strategies that invite all parents to participate in their children's education. By fostering strong partnerships between parents, schools, and communities, we can create supportive environments that promote student success and well-being.

By integrating these strategies, parents can create a supportive and enriching environment that fosters academic and personal growth. Together, we can create a world where every child is surrounded by advocates at home, in school, and in the community.

Equity is everyday work. It looks like offering forms in more than one language, meetings at accessible times, and resources written in plain language. It looks like asking who is missing from the room, then changing the plan so they can come in. Removing friction where families feel it most is practical leadership that honors the dignity of every child.

As I moved deeper into program design, I found myself returning to one simple approach for building bridges among students, families, and staff. First, we build belonging through small rituals that protect the voice. Then we teach simple state tools, such as a long exhale and a grounding movement. We ask what lies beneath the behavior before deciding what to do about it. We co-create one routine to run for two weeks, and we track one or two meaningful measures. Finally, we share what worked and make it easier for the next classroom to try. This cycle keeps us human and accountable at the same time.

I have seen this play out in many rooms. A veteran teacher tried a 60-second pause before discipline, and a student who normally stormed out stayed. A bilingual family night replaced slides with tables of picture books, and parents discovered they were already their child's best reading coach. A fifth grader taught the Captain Cortex lesson to his class and signed off with a sentence I still repeat. You are not bad at focus. Your brain is learning how. None of these moments made headlines, yet each of them changed the climate of a room.

THE POWER TO CHANGE LIVES

From tracing letters in the dust to writing books that bridge cultures. From feeling unseen to helping children feel seen. From surviving the challenges of a post-war time to planting seeds of learning. This is my journey.

Education is not only about tests and textbooks. It is about love, connection, and a steady belief that every child can rise.

When we unlock the power of learning, we unlock the power to change lives. I still picture my grandmother's raincoat book bag. I think of my father in a long line with a form in his hand. I think of Mrs. Jones, of William, of a bilingual book that built a bridge when I needed one. I carry those bridges with me into every classroom. Impact is rarely loud. It is steady, kind, and repeatable. That is how lives change, one small crossing at a time.

References

Dweck, C. S. (2006). Mindset: The New Psychology of Success. Random House.

Edwards, P. A. (2004). Tapping the Potential of Parents: A Strategic Guide to Boosting Student Achievement Through Family Involvement. Scholastic.

Gottman, J., & Declaire, J. (1997). Raising an Emotionally Intelligent Child: The Heart of Parenting. Simon & Schuster.

Morris, A. S., Silk, J. S., Steinberg, L., Myers, S. S., & Robinson, L. R. (2007). The role of the family context in the development of emotion regulation. Social Development, 16(2), 361–388.

Porges, S. W. (2011). The Polyvagal Theory: Neurophysiological Foundations of Emotions, Attachment, Communication, and Self-regulation. W. W. Norton & Company.

Schore, A. N. (2001). The effects of early relational trauma on right brain development, affect regulation, and infant mental health. Infant Mental Health Journal, 22(1-2), 201–269.

Siegel, D. J., & Hartzell, M. (2012). Parenting from the Inside Out: How a Deeper Self-Understanding Can Help You Raise Children Who Thrive. TarcherPerigee.

Sousa, D. A. (2011). How the Brain Learns (4th ed.). Corwin Press. Additional educational research and program details referenced from:

- Families and Schools Together (FAST) Program
- Catalyst Learning Project, Australia
- Aspirnaut STEM Pipeline Program

KIMLY HOANG-NAKATA, M.ED.

Kimly Hoang-Nakata is an award-winning author & educator, MindSmart specialist, learning success coach, global keynote speaker, and CEO/founder of Achieve Education, a coaching service empowering TK–12th grade students through the neuroscience-informed MindSmart Learning Program. She earned international impact recognition for her self-help handbook, *The Glow: How to Lead with Light and Live with Purpose. A Woman's Guide for Sustainable Success*! Her short story collection, *MindSmart Stories for Kids*, gives children the tools to manage big emotions with confidence.

Her bilingual children's picture books, such as *Bringing in Tét, Bringing in the Mid-Autumn Moon Festival, Grandma's Bánh of Love, Mai's Story of Áo Dài: A Bilingual Story of Cultural Beauty and Tradition* celebrate Vietnamese culture and have earned international recognition and First Place BookFest Awards.

Her work has been featured on Global Thought Leaders TV, Times Square, New York City, NBC 7 News, French Chronicles Media,

Peercite Journal of Women Leadership & Mental Health, The New York Times Magazine & WINSPIRE Magazine.

Kimly has received the Exceptional Educator of Excellence and Inspirational Teacher Award from NBC 7 News and was named a 2025 Finalist for Author of the Year in Inspirational Children's Fiction. Blending science with heart, she brings learning to life through stories that inspire growth, resilience, and leadership.

Kimly continues to teach, mentor, and uplift the next generation—with compassion, creativity, and courage.

www.Achieve.education
LinkedIn: *www.linkedin.com/in/Kimly-H-443860349*

RESILIENCE REDEFINED: LEADING THROUGH LIFE'S LABYRINTH

BY DR. MARLINE C. DUROSEAU

FOUNDER & CEO OF MCD BUSINESS ENTERPRISE LLC & ANGEL'S GRACE FOUNDATION, TEDX SPEAKER, AWARD-WINNING AUTHOR, LEADERSHIP & FINANCIAL EXECUTIVE, CPA, MENTOR, RESILIENCE EXPERT, FERTILITY COACH & ADVOCATE, & YOUTH EMPOWERMENT ADVOCATE

My journey to leadership has been anything but traditional. As a woman balancing the current pressures of being a C-suite executive (Chief Financial Officer), a budding entrepreneur (MCD Business Enterprise LLC), Founder & CEO (Angel's Grace Foundation, Inc), a fertility coach and advocate, goal-completion expert and an advocate for women's empowerment, my path has been defined by resilience, transformation, and a deep commitment to creating safe spaces for others to thrive.

One of the most profound experiences of my life has been navigating infertility, a journey that many women face in silence. For me, infertility wasn't just a personal challenge—it became the catalyst for discovering a deeper, more empathetic approach to leadership. As I struggled to conceive and grow my family, I found my voice not only in advocating for my own well-being but also in supporting other women who were facing similar challenges. It's through this journey that I learned that leadership isn't about having all the answers—it's about creating space for others to share their stories, confront their obstacles, and find their strength.

Reaching the C-Suite to become the Chief Financial Officer of an organization after starting off as a payroll coordinator came with its fair share of twists, turns, hard work, dedication, disruption, and transformation. I went from working with others in the organization to accomplish my assigned tasks to leading a team of 30 direct reports and up to 60 overall.

Although leadership is a role I was destined to fulfill, actually occupying the role of a leader with many people looking to me for guidance has been challenging and rewarding. As almost nothing in life comes without unexpected challenges, leadership has taught me to stay the course in order to get myself and those around me to the optimal finish line.

In addition to my corporate roles, coaching, and community advocacy work, I am also a Doctoral research scholar. My research centered around the lived infertility experience of women in leadership roles. This research, which has never been explored in such depth, has the potential to make a lasting impact on the scholarly, clinical, and leadership communities.

By shedding light on the unique challenges faced by women who are striving to build families while navigating leadership roles, my work stands to influence policies, corporate strategies, and the ways in which we understand the intersection of personal and professional challenges.

Through both my personal and professional lived experiences, I have come to realize that leadership is not about fitting into a box—it's about embracing who you are, overcoming adversity, and using your story to inspire others to lead with confidence and resilience. This chapter is a reflection of that journey and the lessons I've learned along the way.

OVERCOMING CHALLENGES

The path to leadership, for me, has never been about a smooth, uninterrupted path. It has always been a journey of navigating adversity, pivoting in real time, and leading with resilience. My story is defined by a series of challenges, each of which has reshaped my approach to leadership.

For most of my life, I was driven by the desire to prove myself, to overcome the hurdles that seemed insurmountable, especially the challenge of infertility. For many years, I was on a path to success defined by outward achievements: a fulfilling career, a growing family, and the recognition of my peers. But the true test of leadership came when things didn't go according to plan.

After starting my senior year of college as an undergraduate, I was not quite clear on which industry I wanted to work in as a Business Management major. As such, I sought out various positions by applying through the college's career office. After sending in multiple applications with no response for about three weeks, I received a surge of interview requests from several companies for Management and Management Trainee positions. I was left to choose between three companies after interviewing for these roles.

I ultimately decided to accept the position of payroll coordinator for a skilled nursing healthcare company. The task of juggling my personal and professional life began on a larger scale at that time, as I was responsible for ensuring that over 350 employees were paid while the looming deadline of graduating from college hovered over me. With the help of my boss and the administration, who eventually became my mentors, I was able to strike a balance and juggle both roles to my satisfaction despite their overlap and the hectic nature of the job.

Infertility was a challenge I never expected, and it became a defining moment in my life. In the face of a diagnosis that would limit my ability to conceive biologically, I had to reckon with my own identity. As a woman leader, I'd always been told that I could "have it all," but this experience challenged that narrative. My career success, my personal dreams of motherhood, and my ambition all collided. I graduated with my Bachelor's as planned. Accomplishing this opened doors for additional opportunities to grow in my professional career.

My boss tested my ability to take on more and grow as a leader by unexpectedly assigning more work or special projects I had no idea how I was going to complete, let alone do correctly and on time. Through these surprise tasks and project assignments, my leadership and strategic thinking skills shone through. I earned multiple promotions, catapulting me further and further into the leadership net.

Would I really be able to do this? How do I get my own work done while ensuring that those who report to me get theirs done as well? Now I am dealing with infertility! What will happen if my boss finds out? Will they demote me, or even fire me, because they will think I am unable to do the job? How do I explain the time away from the office? I need to attend my doctors' appointments and fertility procedures. This time was beyond stressful to say the least. As such, I over-performed in order to not only get my work done, but also show my job that I was committed and could do the job well despite the secret infertility journey I was on.

However, I realized that the way I responded to this challenge would shape not only my personal journey but also my approach to leadership. It wasn't about overcoming infertility in the traditional sense. Instead, it was about learning to lead through it—accepting that I couldn't control everything and finding strength in vulnerability. I found solace in opening up to others, in sharing my struggles with peers who understood the weight of what I was going through, and in showing up for my team, clients, and family, despite my own uncertainty.

Infertility was one of the first major obstacles I faced, a deeply personal battle that tested my endurance and determination. While navigating this journey, I also found myself leading through a global crisis, COVID-19. As the world shut down, businesses scrambled to adapt, and leaders were expected to make swift, often unprecedented decisions. There was no rulebook, no precedent for managing a team, adjusting strategies, and maintaining morale in the face of so much uncertainty.

During that time, my team faced significant turnover, leaving fewer resources to help us achieve the goals we had set. Yet, in this crisis, I learned one of the most important lessons of my leadership career: when there is no clear path forward, it's up to you to create one. I was forced to make tough calls, shift priorities, and find ways to keep my team motivated and moving forward. The key was not only staying adaptable but also communicating openly with my team and maintaining a sense of hope, even when things seemed bleak.

By leading through both infertility and the COVID-19 crisis, I learned that leadership isn't defined by perfection—it's about resilience, adaptability, and the courage to make difficult decisions in times of uncertainty. Through this experience, I began to reshape my understanding of leadership—not as the pursuit of perfection, but as a continual process of growth, empathy, and authenticity.

VALUES & DECISION-MAKING:
YOUR LEADERSHIP BLUEPRINT

A key principle that has always guided me throughout my leadership journey is the value of continuous learning and education. Raised by immigrant parents who placed immense value on education, I internalized the belief that knowledge is power—and that education doesn't stop once you leave school. This value has been my compass, especially as I worked to grow in my career while navigating infertility and life's many demands.

I earned my Bachelor's, Master's, and CPA License, all while struggling with the personal challenge of infertility. I also chose to pursue my Doctoral degree, all in the midst of juggling my professional responsibilities and personal life. Each degree, each achievement wasn't just a step forward in my career. It was a deliberate act of ensuring that I had the knowledge, skills, and authority to make the right decisions in both my professional and personal life.

Additionally, the concept of leadership being empowerment helped guide me through some of the toughest moments. I've always been driven by a deep desire to help others rise above their challenges. Whether it's mentoring a woman in her career, helping women and youth set goals and achieve them, or providing emotional support to someone going through their own fertility journey, I've built my leadership style around these values.

As I progressed through my career and began to navigate the complexities of infertility, I had to make hard decisions that aligned with my values. One of the toughest choices was whether to continue pursuing a high-powered career while trying to manage the emotional and physical toll of infertility. I quickly realized that my health and happiness had to come first. I started setting stronger boundaries, creating space for self-care, and being honest with myself and others about what I could and couldn't handle.

The decision to invest in my own well-being, both mentally and physically, was one of the most impactful leadership choices I've ever made. I saw firsthand how self-care impacts not only your own life but your ability to lead and empower others. It taught me that leadership isn't about pushing through at all costs. It's about knowing when to step back, prioritize, and show up as the best version of yourself.

Through every challenge I faced, whether infertility, career growth, or leading during crises, education has provided me with the tools to pivot, evolve, and continue growing. It's a value I carry with me in everything I do, reminding me that there is always room to learn, to grow, and to better myself as a leader.

CREATING IMPACT:
MENTORSHIP, ADVOCACY, & EMPOWERMENT

Leadership is not just about making decisions—it's about creating a legacy of change and empowerment. I've always been driven by the desire to not only succeed personally but to elevate others along the way. This is why I have dedicated much of my career to mentorship and advocacy, particularly in the realm of infertility.

My journey from infertility to leadership has been a testament to the importance of mentorship and advocacy. I have spent much of my career helping others achieve their potential, whether in my role as a CFO, a coach, or a mentor to younger women and future leaders. Through my work, I've created a ripple effect of change in both the business world and personal lives.

I am proud to be an official fertility advocate with RESOLVE, a national organization dedicated to supporting those affected by infertility. As a fertility coach and advocate, I've seen firsthand the importance of advocacy in creating meaningful change. Through my work as a Doctoral Research Scholar at National University, I led a groundbreaking research initiative that explored the experiences of women in leadership roles who are also facing infertility.

This research, the first of its kind, has the potential to significantly change how the world views women in leadership and infertility. My conceptual framework, Leader Morphology in the Labyrinth™, my seminal work and leadership framework, focuses on the morphology of leader identity through the adaptations leaders make after infertility or trauma-informed lived experiences.

Conducting this research and my advocacy work align with my passion for advocating for women in leadership, particularly those facing the unique challenges of infertility. It's a subject that is often overlooked, despite the fact that many women struggle with this issue while simultaneously climbing the corporate ladder or leading organizations. The interviews conducted with the research participants, women in leadership, yielded raw, intimate, and eye-opening firsthand experiences they've had as women leaders dealing with infertility, which can be applied to any disruption leaders face in life. Ultimately, I have found that the essence of leadership includes leader identity morphology, resilience, and the ability to adapt.

My work with the nonprofit organization Filling Empty Wombs has been incredibly fulfilling, as I've been able to not only support women on their fertility journeys but also raise awareness about the emotional and professional challenges they face.

When faced with gaps in support or areas of improvement, I've learned the importance of being proactive and assertive. If something is missing or if it's not perfect, it's up to us to step in and fill the void. In leadership, we are often tasked with trailblazing the way forward. I've learned that leadership isn't just about following established paths; it's about creating new ones for others to follow. The impact I am making through my research and advocacy is not just for me—it's for the next generation of women who will one day lead.

Moreover, I've made it a priority to give back by mentoring young women who aspire to leadership roles. I share my story openly and encourage them to embrace their individuality, regardless of the obstacles they may face. Through mentorship, I've seen firsthand the transformative impact it can have, whether it's helping someone take the next step in their career or simply providing a listening ear when they need it most.

ACTIONABLE TAKEAWAYS:
EMPOWERING READERS TO LEAD

In leadership, there are guiding principles that can empower you not only to overcome challenges but also to thrive in the face of adversity. For me, the core principles that drive my leadership are captured in my MCD framework: Be Motivated, Be Courageous, Be Dynamic.

Be Motivated: Your motivation drives you to push forward, even when the path is unclear. Keep your vision and purpose front and center and allow that motivation to guide you through even the toughest times.

Be Courageous: Leadership often requires making difficult decisions, stepping into uncomfortable spaces, and taking risks. Being courageous isn't about having no fear—it's about acting in spite of it.

Be Dynamic: Leadership isn't static. It requires constant growth, flexibility, and the ability to pivot as needed. Embrace change and use it as a catalyst for transformation, both personally and professionally.

By following these inter-personal principles, you'll be better equipped to lead with confidence, inspire others, and create lasting change in your personal and professional spheres.

Additionally, I want to leave readers with actionable insights they can apply to their own lives, personally and professionally. Leadership is not a one-size-fits-all endeavor—it's a dynamic process that requires self-awareness, resilience, and a commitment to continuous growth.

Here are some of the key takeaways that can help you lead with confidence, even in the face of adversity:

Embrace Vulnerability: Leadership isn't about perfection. It's about showing up authentically and sharing your story. Don't be afraid to let others see the real you—your struggles, your victories, and your journey.

Set Boundaries: Establishing clear boundaries is essential for your well-being and effectiveness as a leader. Protect your time, your mental health, and your energy so you can show up fully for those who rely on you.

Invest in Mentorship: Seek out mentors who will challenge you, support you, and help you grow. The best leaders are those who never stop learning from others. As a mentee, be reminded it is imperative you are coachable to allow those mentoring you to get the messages to you in a manner in which you can receive feedback and the information being provided.

Prioritize Self-Care: You cannot pour from an empty cup. Make self-care a non-negotiable part of your leadership practice. Only when you take care of yourself can you effectively lead others.

Lead with Empathy: Leadership is about understanding the needs and struggles of those around you. Approach every situation with empathy and a willingness to listen.

THE INTERSECTION OF PERSONAL & PROFESSIONAL LEADERSHIP

My journey has shown me that leadership is not confined to the boardroom; it's an integrated part of your life. As a woman who's navigated infertility while leading at the highest levels of business, I understand how challenging it can be to balance your personal aspirations with your professional ambitions. However, I've also learned that embracing the intersection of these two worlds can lead to unparalleled growth.

By acknowledging and respecting my personal journey with infertility, I've become a better leader in the professional world. I approach leadership with greater empathy, understanding that every person is juggling their own challenges. I've learned that the most effective leaders are those who don't compartmentalize their lives but rather bring their whole selves to the table—authenticity, vulnerabilities, and all.

Throughout my journey, I've witnessed the disruption that can occur in our lives, especially when personal challenges intersect with our professional responsibilities. These disruptions often push us off the course we thought we were on and challenge the duality of our personal and professional roles. For women, this intersection is particularly poignant. We are expected to succeed both at home and at work. Yet the realities of life often demand that we adapt and shift between these roles, sometimes unexpectedly.

Rather than fighting against these disruptions, I've learned to embrace them. The challenges we face, whether infertility, loss, or the upheaval of a global pandemic, don't have to derail our leadership journey. Instead, they can serve as moments of growth and evolution. We are made to adapt, to change, and to allow the intersection of our personal and professional lives to coexist, even when it feels messy or overwhelming.

Your purpose, what you were made to do, is rooted in your ability to help others. Don't let the disruptions of life make you abandon your goals. Instead, let them propel you toward your purpose, allowing the intersection of your personal and professional journeys to create a path forward uniquely yours.

INSPIRING THE NEXT GENERATION OF LEADERS

As leaders, it's our responsibility to pave the way for the next generation, inspiring, guiding, and supporting those who will follow. For the next generation of leaders, I offer this advice: seek out mentors, remain coachable, stay open-minded, and believe in your abilities. The road to leadership is not always easy, and it often requires flexibility, open-mindedness, and a willingness to grow.

But it also requires confidence—confidence in your abilities, in your vision, and in your potential to create change. Don't be afraid to seek help when you need it. No one can lead alone; great leaders recognize the value of mentorship, community, and support.

The next generation of leaders will face their own unique challenges. My hope is that by sharing my story and the lessons I've learned, I can help inspire them to step into their power, lead with courage, and make a lasting impact on the world around them. As I look ahead, I am inspired by the countless leaders—especially women—who are stepping into their power, breaking through barriers, and paving the way for others. I want my story to be one of encouragement: no matter the challenges you face, you have the power to lead with impact and influence. Leadership is not a destination, but a journey. Embrace the obstacles, learn from them, and use your experiences to empower others.

In the words of one of my favorite mentors, "Leadership is about creating the next generation of leaders." I am committed to doing just that, whether through my coaching, my writing, or the work I do every day to support women in leadership. We are all capable of leading, no matter what our circumstances. I hope my story serves as a reminder that leadership is not defined by what we've overcome, but by how we choose to use our experiences to uplift others.

Just always remember to Be Motivated, Be Courageous, and Be Dynamic while doing it!

DR. MARLINE C. DUROSEAU

Dr. Marline C. Duroseau is a seasoned leadership executive with over 23 years of experience in finance and management. Holding a Certified Public Accountant (CPA) license, she has ascended through various corporate roles, demonstrating resilience and a commitment to excellence. Marline is also a doctoral researcher and scholar, focusing her research on women's infertility and leadership, aiming to contribute valuable insights to this underexplored field.

In her memoir, *It'll Happen by 30: A Relentless Journey of Faith Delayed But Not Denied*, Marline candidly shares her decade-long struggle with infertility and child loss. The book serves as a beacon of hope for others facing similar challenges, providing raw honesty and empathy.

Beyond writing, Marline is a fervent advocate for women's empowerment. She founded MCD Business Enterprise LLC, dedicated to building confidence among women and supporting them in balancing career ambitions with personal aspirations.

A Miami native and daughter of Haitian immigrants, Marline has been married to her husband, Kevens, for over 23 years. Together, they have four sons: Richard, twins Kason and Kamden, and Kevens Benjamin (KB). The family actively engages in community and church activities, reflecting Marline's belief in service and giving back.

Marline's commitment to service is evident through her roles as Chairperson for the Finance Committee at the Church of the Visitation of the Blessed Virgin Mary and as Treasurer for her local Homeowners' Association. She also serves as an Ambassador, CFO, and Board Member for the nonprofit organization Filling Empty Wombs, advocating for those navigating fertility challenges.

Dr. Marline C. Duroseau exemplifies resilience, leadership, and a steadfast commitment to empowering others, particularly women facing fertility challenges.

www.MCDBE.com
LinkedIn: *www.linkedin.com/in/MCDBE*

LEAD WITH HEART: HOW I TURNED PAIN INTO PURPOSE & BUILT A BUSINESS THAT CHANGES LIVES

BY MELISSA MONJARAZ

SENIOR LOAN OFFICER, HOME LOAN WIZARD, AUTHOR,
& TEAM LEAD OF HOMELOANSWITHMELISSA
AT LEGACY MUTUAL MORTGAGE

THE STORY OF A FIRST-GEN LATINA

If someone had told me back in 2003 that I'd be ranked in the top 1% of loan officers in the nation, leading a powerhouse mortgage team, and changing lives every single day, I wouldn't have believed them.

Back then, I had just moved from Santa Cruz, California, to Chandler, Arizona. The plan was to finish college at ASU and become an accountant, but the universe had other plans. I took a job as a receptionist at a local mortgage company. Within six months, I was promoted to loan officer, and the moment I started helping families get into homes, I knew I had found my calling.

I never imagined I'd be where I am today. I fell in love with helping people achieve their dream of homeownership, especially those who never thought it was possible. Over time, I realized this was more than just a job. It became a mission to build something meaningful and make a real impact, one family at a time.

When people meet me today, they see my success. They see the awards, the rankings, the business I've built. But what they don't see —what most people never hear—is where it all started.

I grew up in Santa Cruz, California, in a place called The Villa San Carlos. It was a tight-knit Latino community where many families faced real struggles. We lived in low-income housing, and while there was a strong sense of community and resilience all around us, there were also challenges, like gangs, drugs, and uncertainty.

As a child, I witnessed things no kid should have to see, and our small apartment was often crowded and unpredictable. But I have no regrets—some of my closest, lifelong friends came from those early days, and the experiences I had there shaped who I am. They gave me the drive to build a different future and the heart to help others do the same.

My dad, an immigrant from Aguascalientes, Mexico, came to the U.S. when he was just 14 years old. He did the best he could with what he knew and worked tirelessly to provide for our family. He owned a small business—Auto Spa of California, a car detail shop— and spent long hours building it, so we never went without. My mom helped out by cleaning houses here and there, but her full-time job was raising all five of us kids.

With so many of us and both of them focused on giving us a better life, it wasn't easy for them to catch everything happening at home. My older brothers got involved with gangs and drugs, and while that became part of our reality, I always felt something deep inside pulling me in a different direction—toward something more.

Even in the most dysfunctional environments, I stayed focused. I got good grades. I poured my energy into cheerleading, dance, and friendships that gave me a glimpse of a different life.

My best friend, Valeria Flores, and her family became my "second family"—they even call me "la hija adoptada." They brought structure, discipline, and positive influence that shaped me. Sure, we had our moments of sneaking out and mischief, but mostly it was fun and kept me out of trouble. I'm grateful for their love and guidance.

Like many who grow up in tough neighborhoods, I experienced things that were difficult and heavy to carry. Things that shaped me, challenged me, and forced me to grow up earlier than I should have. What I've learned is that your past doesn't have to define you, but it can refine you. It can build compassion. It can sharpen your drive. And it can become the very fuel you use to make a difference in the lives of others.

A lot of what I know about entrepreneurship, I learned from my dad. He ran his own business, worked tirelessly, and always said, "If you want to be successful, you have to work for yourself." That mindset took root in me early on and continues to shape the way I approach my career. I'd watch how he connected with people—he'd take time to ask questions, listen, and build real relationships.

To this day, some of his customers still stop by just to catch up with him. He also taught me the value of making memories. Some of my favorite moments growing up were our lake trips, family dirt bike rides, and visits to Mexico to see my grandparents.

From my mom, I learned patience and kindness. She's the most honest, selfless, and forgiving person I know. Those qualities have deeply influenced how I show up in my business—with empathy, transparency, and a genuine desire to help.

My parents did the best they could with what they had, but like many families in our community, we faced real challenges. Despite all their hard work, they never had the chance to buy a home in California. My dad always said he could have bought a home we rented for $40,000, never did, and that home is now worth 1.2 million. That became a driving force for me. Years later, I had the honor of helping them secure a home loan for them to purchase their first home in

Arizona—and that moment shaped my mission to help other families do the same.

Each of my siblings chose a different path—some took the wrong turn, others built something solid for themselves, and I am super proud of them. We all handled our upbringing in our own way. And me?

I chose to *break the cycle.*

I chose to rise.

I knew I wanted a different life. A life filled with peace, purpose, and impact. And even though I didn't know exactly how to get there, I knew one thing for sure:

My past was not going to define my future.

I wasn't going to let my environment, my circumstances, or anyone's choices dictate what was possible for me. I wanted to build something beautiful out of the broken pieces.

And that's exactly what I set out to do.

BUILDING, BREAKING, & RISING AGAIN

After everything I had been through in my early years, I thought the hard part was over.

But life had more lessons for me—lessons in humility, partnership, and perseverance.

In **2005**, Hory—my boyfriend at the time, now my husband—and I started working together. We were young, ambitious, and full of energy: just two people with big dreams and no idea of the storm that was ahead.

By 2006, we took a leap and opened our own mortgage office.

At first, it felt like we were finally stepping into our moment. The business grew quickly, and so did our confidence. But then came the collapse.

Everyone remembers the 2008 housing crash, but what many forget is that the ground started crumbling in 2007. We felt it firsthand. Deals dried up. Clients disappeared. Banks went out of business. We couldn't keep the lights on. We were working twice as hard for barely enough to get by.

Eventually, we had to let go of everything, including the four homes we had worked so hard to acquire. We lost them all.

We filed for bankruptcy.

We had no money. No cars. No home.

We moved in with my mom in Chandler, Arizona, and borrowed her car. My parents didn't charge us rent, which was a huge help— family is everything, and we were fortunate to have them during this difficult time. My mother-in-law, Martha, gave us gas gift cards and food credit cards. It was humbling, heartbreaking, and heavy. Although my in-laws repeatedly offered financial assistance, we insisted on standing on our own.

We were completely stripped down to nothing, financially and emotionally. And to be honest, there was a moment when we almost gave up entirely. We had people close to us saying, *"Maybe real estate just isn't for you."*

But I'm not wired to quit.

I told Hory, "Let's give it one more go. What happened wasn't just us —it happened to the world."

So we started over. We decided to get our real estate license and joined a real estate team in 2008. At first, the commissions were small—$2,000 per deal, if that. And the work was endless. We were nickel-and-diming for survival, counting gas cards and grocery coupons. There were days when we truly had nothing. Just a $1 to our name. I remember having to split a Whopper from Burger King when they were $1.

But we kept going.

We showed up for the opportunity even when it didn't show up for us.

And little by little, we rebuilt. We got organized. We created systems. We learned how to run our business, not just hustle inside of it. And most importantly, we kept our faith in each other—and, in the future, we remained determined to create.

Because the truth is, **your rock bottom can become your foundation—if you don't give up.**

That year taught me more than any mentor, class, or book ever could. It taught me that leadership doesn't start when things are easy. It starts when everything falls apart, and you still choose to rise.

THE MOMENT EVERYTHING CHANGED

After we filed for bankruptcy, after we lost every home we had… There was this quiet moment. I still remember it like it was yesterday.

It was just the two of us—Hory and I—sitting at this little table upstairs in my mom's house. We had nothing but each other, some school transcripts, and one big question hanging in the air:

"Do we quit or do we keep going?"

We talked about going back to school. Hory considered business and marketing. I had always thought about becoming an accountant. And for a second, it felt like maybe that would be the easier route—start over completely, walk away from the pain of what had collapsed.

But then we looked at each other and realized something: **we still believed in what we could build.**

We knew how hard we had worked. We knew the market had crashed —it wasn't just us. It happened to people across the country. So we made a decision that day:

We're not going to quit. We're going to go all in.

And this time, we're doing it with 100% focus.

Everything changed from that moment forward.

We stopped going out. We stopped chasing distractions. No drinking. No social circles. No late nights. Just work and health. That was the rhythm: **Work. Gym. Sleep. Repeat.**

And it wasn't easy. We were rebuilding from scratch, scraping together gas money and grocery gift cards. But what we had, finally, was *clarity*. We cut out anything that wasn't aligned with our vision—and that included the people around us.

We learned quickly that not everyone is meant to go where you're going.

Some people only support you when you're down. Others resurface when you rise. I had someone tell me, "Now that you're having success, you think you're too good for us." And the answer in my head was simple: I didn't change. My *standards* did.

When you're building something meaningful—especially from nothing—you learn that instant gratification isn't worth the long-term cost. We chose **sacrifice over shortcuts, discipline over distractions, and vision over validation.**

And that's when everything started to turn around.

THE START OF SOMETHING BIGGER THAN ME

From the very beginning, I knew this wasn't just about real estate or loans—it was about people. About their first home. Their dream kitchen. The neighborhood where their kids would ride bikes. I saw the impact we could make, and I made a decision: every client would be treated like family. Every file would matter. Every dream would be honored.

It's why I do what I do today. Because I know what it's like to grow up in a home where **the dream of owning a house felt out of reach.** I know how intimidating the system can feel when no one explains it to you in your language or with patience. So now, every time I sit across from a first-time homebuyer, especially a Latino family, I see my own story in theirs—and I make sure they feel seen, heard, and supported.

Being a first-gen Latina didn't just shape how I see the world.

It shaped how I lead in it.

In 2012, I decided to return full-time to mortgages—because helping families with home loans has always been my true passion. I joined a top-producing mortgage team and continued to grow. By 2017, I felt ready to branch out and launch my mortgage team. Today, I'm proud to be ranked as a **Top loan officer** in the country and among the **top 250 Latino lenders nationwide.** But titles don't define me—service does.

I show up every day for my clients, my team, and my family with one mantra in mind:

"Quitting is not an option."

BUILDING A BUSINESS & A LIFE I LOVE

I wouldn't be where I am today without my husband, Hory. He's not just my marriage partner—he's my business partner, in vision, in growth, and in life. He is my biggest cheerleader and has always believed in me.

Together, we've built more than a mortgage business.

We've built a life—anchored in love, shaped by resilience, and fueled by a shared mission to help families create wealth through homeownership.

But let me be clear: it hasn't always been easy.

Working with your spouse means you're not just sharing a desk—you're sharing pressure, financial risks, late nights, tough decisions, and emotional highs and lows. There were seasons we struggled—really struggled. There were moments we barely had enough money for food, gas, let alone business growth. We had to lean on each other, trust each other, and recommit—sometimes daily—to building not just the business, but the relationship behind it.

Here's what we learned along the way—and what I want every aspiring leader, entrepreneur, Mom, and couple to know:

1. Communication is Everything

You can't run a business together if you can't talk honestly. We had to learn how to separate the personal from the professional —how to give feedback without making it personal, and how to speak up without shutting the other person down. Every success in our business was built on a foundation of *open* and *respectful communication.*

2. Define Your Roles

At one point, we were trying to do everything together. That led to tension, confusion, and burnout. Eventually, we sat down and clarified who was responsible for what. I focused on client relationships, deals, and leadership. Hory focused on operations, back-end systems, and business growth strategy. We stayed in our zones of genius, and the business started to flow.

3. Prioritize Your Family—Always

The biggest win of our lives isn't the business. It's our son, Luca. Becoming parents gave us an even deeper sense of purpose. Everything we do—every loan we close, every family we serve—it's all to build a legacy for him. We want Luca to grow up watching two parents who lead with love, make an impact, and never back down from their dreams.

4. Redefining Success Through My Son's Eyes

Luca taught me that success isn't just hitting numbers—it's about living your values. He sees me work hard and then switch gears to spend quality time at home. He watches me push through challenges and apologize when I miss bedtime. Letting him know he comes first reminds me that success involves love, not just income.

Knowing your child's love language is important. I have learned that Luca's love language is **_Quality Time_**. I focus on that one thing instead of buying him gifts, as he just wants me to be present. I celebrate team wins and family milestones because a fulfilled life and a thriving business go hand in hand.

5. Your Business Should Support Your Life—Not Consume It

There's a misconception in entrepreneurship that success means hustling 24/7, never sleeping, never pausing. I believed that for a while, too. But I've learned that real success means building a business that supports your life, not the other way around. Yes, we work hard. But we also build in rest, family time, and fun. Because a burned-out leader can't build a sustainable business. And an overwhelmed parent can't be fully present at home. It's not perfect, but we work at it every day.

6. Finding My Confidence in a Crowd

When I went to my first coaching summit in 2019, I walked into a room with about 500 top mortgage experts, mostly men. There were hardly any women, and even fewer Latina women like me. I felt nervous and out of place. I kept thinking, "Can I do this? Am I smart enough? Do I belong here?" I wondered, "What if they knew where I came from—would they judge me?" Watching those people go on stage and close big deals made me feel small.

Lesson: Even when you're the only one who looks like you, don't let it stop you. Your story and background are strengths, not weaknesses. Everyone has doubts, but believing in yourself is what makes you stand out.

So, when people ask me what I'm most proud of, I say this:

Not just the homes we've financed.

Not just the awards or top 1% status.

But the life we've built—intentionally, wholeheartedly, and side by side.

We've created something meaningful because we never gave up on ourselves, on each other, or on the families we serve.

And if we can do it, **you can too.**

You don't have to choose between a successful business and a fulfilling family life.

You can build both—with the right mindset, support, and commitment.

Start where you are. Grow through what you go through. And lead every part of your life with love and purpose. That's what it means to build a business—and a life—you truly love.

GROWTH IS A CHOICE

I believe all great leadership begins with leading yourself first. That's why I've committed deeply to personal growth and development over the years. I've had the privilege of learning from some of the best, like Tony Robbins and the elite coaching company for realtors and lenders at **The CORE**. I also completed **Forward Academy**, where I learned how to blend technology, AI, and video to better educate today's modern homebuyers. I chose to align myself with a company led by top-producing mortgage professionals and industry mentors. One thing I've learned through it all: *who you work with truly matters.* That's why I've made it a priority to surround myself with the best in the business.

In this fast-changing world, staying stagnant isn't an option. I constantly challenge myself to grow so I can better serve my team, my clients, and my community.

LEADING THROUGH CONNECTION

In today's digital world, I believe social media is a powerful tool for impact—but only when it's used with intention. For me, platforms like Instagram are not about flashy content or sales. They're about education, connection, and empowerment.

I share my story so others can see what's possible. I break down the home loan process so first-time buyers can feel confident. I celebrate client wins because they remind me why I do this work in the first place. I share family time and the real me.

I've learned that when you lead with authenticity, people don't just follow—you earn their trust. And through that genuine connection, I've been able to build some of the most meaningful friendships on Instagram. It's become such a powerful way to connect with like-minded people who share the same passion and purpose.

WHY I DO WHAT I DO

At the heart of it all, this business is deeply personal to me. Every loan I close represents a dream realized. A chapter opened. A new beginning for someone who trusted me to guide them there.

I've helped more than a thousand families step into homeownership, but I treat every single one like it's the first. I never forget how overwhelming the process can feel. That's why I take the time to listen, educate, and walk my clients through each step with patience and care.

This isn't just about getting a loan—it's about building a foundation for a lifetime.

THE IMPACT I WANT TO LEAVE

If there's one thing I've learned, it's that **real leadership is about lifting others up.**

Whether I'm mentoring my team, serving my clients, or raising my son, I want to be remembered as someone who led with *heart*. Someone who turned challenges into opportunities, and opportunities into impact.

I want women in this industry to know they can *rise*. I want First Gen Latinas to know they, too, can be successful. I want first-time buyers to know they *can own*. I want my community to know that no matter where you start, you can *build a life beyond anything you imagined.*

My journey—from receptionist to top loan officer—isn't just my story. It's proof that with belief, mentorship, grit, and love, anything is possible.

And I've learned that when you lead with authenticity, people don't just follow you—they trust you, and I can now say that I have built some of the most beautiful friendships through Instagram. It is a powerful tool to meet other like-minded people.

WHY I DO WHAT I DO

At the heart of it all, this business is deeply personal to me. Every loan I close represents a dream realized. A chapter opened. A new beginning for someone who trusted me to guide them there.

I've helped more than a thousand families step into homeownership, but I treat every single one like it's the first. I never forget how overwhelming the process can feel. That's why I take the time to listen, educate, and walk my clients through each step with patience and care.

This isn't just about getting a loan—it's about building a foundation for a lifetime.

THE IMPACT I WANT TO LEAVE

If there's one thing I've learned, it's that **real leadership is about lifting others.**

Whether I'm mentoring my team, serving my clients, or raising my son, I want to be remembered as someone who led with *heart*. Someone who turned challenges into opportunities, and opportunities into impact.

I want women in this industry to know they can *rise*. I want first-time buyers to know they *can own*. I want my community to know that no matter where you start, you can *build a life beyond anything you imagined.*

My journey—from receptionist to top loan officer—isn't just my story. It's proof that with belief, mentorship, grit, and love, anything is possible.

This chapter is my way of giving back. To say: if I can do it, so can you.

Let's keep leading. Let's keep growing. And let's keep making an impact—one family, one home, and one dream at a time.

YOUR STORY ISN'T OVER—IT'S JUST GETTING STARTED

If there's one thing I hope you take away from my story, it's this: You don't need perfect circumstances to become a leader. You don't need the right connections, background, or bank account. You just need the courage to say, "I'm not going to let where I come from define where I'm going." I came from the projects. From chaos. From dysfunction. I had every reason to quit—more than once. I lost everything. I failed. I started over. And then I rose again. And I'm still rising. Not because I'm special, but because I made a decision:

I wasn't going to wait for someone to hand me a dream. I was going to build one.

If you're reading this right now and you feel stuck, unsure, or overwhelmed by your circumstances, please know this:

You already have everything inside of you to create the life you dream about.

You don't need permission. You need *conviction*.

Be the leader in your own life. Show up when no one's clapping. Work when no one's watching. Speak your vision out loud, even when your voice shakes.

There will be people who doubt you. There will be moments when you doubt yourself. But the ones who succeed—the ones who make a real impact—are the ones who choose to take the next step anyway.

You were never meant to play small. You were never meant to blend in. You were meant to rise, to lead, and to show others what's possible. And if no one has told you lately, let me be the first: **You are worthy. You are capable. And you're ready.**

Start where you are. Use what you have. And lead with heart. Your impact begins the moment you decide to own your story— and take action toward the life you were born to live. The world needs more leaders. The world needs more dreamers who do. The world needs **you.**

So go out there and make it happen.

MELISSA MONJARAZ

Melissa Monjaraz is an experienced Senior Mortgage Loan Officer at Legacy Mutual Mortgage, based in Arizona. With over a decade of experience in the mortgage and real estate industry, she specializes in helping individuals and families navigate the complexities of securing home financing.

Melissa is skilled in various areas, including U.S. VA Loans, FHA loans, foreclosures, and relocation services. Her extensive expertise in these fields allows her to guide clients through the mortgage process with confidence, ensuring they receive the best possible financing options.

She is passionate about working with first-time homebuyers and has built a reputation for her commitment to customer service, always ensuring that each client feels informed and supported throughout the loan process. Melissa is also fluent in both English and Spanish, which allows her to serve a wider range of clients and help bridge communication gaps in the home-buying process.

Melissa holds both a Real Estate License and an Arizona Mortgage License from the Arizona School of Real Estate and Business, providing her with the qualifications needed to help clients with their home financing needs.

With her strong commitment to excellence and customer satisfaction, Melissa continues to be a trusted professional in the mortgage industry, assisting clients with achieving their homeownership goals.

www.TheMonjarazTeam.Floify.com
Instagram: *@homeloanswithmelissa*

THE FORMULA FOR SUCCESS

BY NATIA KHADURI

REMARKABLE AUTHOR, MATHEMATICIAN, LAW &
INTERNATIONAL RELATIONS EXPERT, POET, & PROSE
WRITER

"Love is the only thing that you spend and multiply."

My life path is akin to a fairy tale, a magical journey for a young girl and a profound discovery for a woman. It all began with the enchanting world of literature. It is how the story unfolded:

When my older sister and the children in the neighbourhood went to the village library to subscribe to books, they took me. I carefully chose children's books or magazines, but didn't dare say I also wanted to subscribe to a book. But there was no other way; I had to say it because the others would soon finish their work. This was the beginning of my deep love for literature, a love that would shape my life in ways I couldn't yet imagine.

"Aunt Nato, I want a book too," I told the librarian, my eyes shining. I was five years old at the time, and I was going to kindergarten. Aunt Nato was amazed by my enthusiasm and good reading and writing skills at a young age; she helped me choose a fairy tale. Finally, she said she would sign the book subscription document for me. I said, "I'll write it," and grabbed a pen. I was a big kid and could ideally get to Aunt Nato's desk. I had a magazine-sized book,

"Khutkunchula," in my hand, and I ran down the hill breathlessly to show my mother my first independent "discovery" and share the tale.

Thus, my life's tale began, filled with more challenges and intentional hurt than joy. Yet, in the end, it was always the triumph of resilience and determination, often fueled by the stories I read. The characters in those books became my companions, teaching me about courage, perseverance, and hope. They inspired me to keep going, to never give up, no matter how difficult the circumstances.

When I was admitted to school, I knew the first-grade material by heart. My childhood was entirely covered by that "period of darkness," and even finding and reading a book meant a lot of effort. Back then, it was the time of long-term civil war in Georgia, and my country had no electricity, gas, or heating. Sometimes, I even had to ensure that the candle I used to light the dark was still there for the next night. There was no Internet then, and even watching movies on TV was a great luxury and an expensive life for me. There wasn't a big selection of children's books in my family. That may be why I started reading novels in the first grade. I would choose books by the "body" and volume, and then read until the candle went out. The civil war brought not only physical challenges but also emotional and mental ones. I won't write more about those difficult days. Instead, I will continue to tell my story by recounting the most difficult days.

My marriage was a union not of my choosing and marked the most agonizing years of my life. At the tender age of 16, I was thrust into a family that forbade me from indulging in my love for books, stripping me of all joy and desire. Despite my best efforts and tears, I managed to enroll in university, a testament to my unwavering determination. Even when forced to abandon my studies, I never lost hope.

When I entered university for the second time, I was 32 years old. I moved to the capital with two children and began fighting for education and personal development. My journey was about academic pursuits, personal growth, and resilience. I studied at the university, balancing my studies with raising my children and working at night. This experience enhanced my academic knowledge and fostered personal growth, teaching me resilience, time management, and the importance of self-discipline. It was a testament to my determination and the transformative power of education in my life. I was happy if I slept two or three hours a day. I worked in a financial organization and was soon promoted to manager because I performed management flawlessly and did accounting brilliantly. At that time, I thought mathematics was my best job. But in 2020, when the pandemic stopped the world globally, I started writing. It was not just a new career path but a reflection of my love for literature and the power of self-expression. I also had surgery five months before the pandemic. They removed both lymph nodes and the thyroid gland from my neck because large nodules had formed, and we ended the subsequent cancerous transformations in this way. It affected me a lot. I wasn't afraid of death, but I regretted my life. I didn't want this to happen at the age of 39.

There are truths you don't want to believe and don't believe. So, I got up and didn't believe that I was facing death. I wrapped my hands around all my writings and, holding my writings in my heart; I left the house. After a great struggle with myself, I also mixed my first poem into the prose sheets, and what excited me most was my first novel. I had to leave nothing out. Everything has its role and purpose in the vast depths of my vision; one way or another, we are connected.

The editor was interested in my writings. "Nothing will be changed today!" I answered in the same tone, because I might not be here tomorrow! "Poetry should come first. Poetry, first of all," Mr. Murad said. "We will say goodbye, and I will wait for your call," I said.

Suddenly, the sound of the phone ringing woke me up. "Yes, Mr. Murad, I hear you...." "You lied to me!" I froze in one place. "I couldn't believe this is your first novel! It is at least your fifth novel." Now, joy made me speechless, and with great effort, I managed to whisper, "Thank you, Mr. Murad, thank you very much."

His words were like a burst of joy: "Even the great classics couldn't write such meaningful and well-written dialogues flawlessly. Congratulations! It is the introduction, the continuation of which will be world classic fiction." I stood stunned with joy, and the only word that could now wipe the tears from my petrified face was, "Thank you!" I said goodbye to him and shouted, "It is out!"

Since that day, my writing and I have been on a journey of self-discovery. I found myself penning a second novel in just a week. And then, a third. This rapid progression marked my growing confidence in my writing and my personal growth. I look at the successes tenderly arranged on my palm, and my heart is touched that they are called "The Road from Home to Emigration."

It was spring 2022. On April 1, I entered the great hall of the National Library of the Parliament of Tbilisi, and with my poetry, I said goodbye to Tbilisi and my dear people. Their embrace accompanied me on the most challenging path, and only the next day, upon arriving in Istanbul, I escaped the euphoria of joy.

I stopped in Istanbul, where the Georgian Cultural Center generously hosted me that night. Thus started the poem *My Path to Emigration*, a reflection of my emotional journey from Tbilisi to America. I was in America soon after leaving Istanbul. The joy the opportunity to fulfil my dream gave me in New York seemed sad. I did not dare to look back for a long time because my homeland stood behind me like a crying child. I avoided this feeling a little when the Georgians gathered in the hall of the first Georgian Center in America—it warmed my soul. I, too, "energized" by their love, wrote poetry and was happy to be in my "homeland."

At first, the challenges come suddenly like an attack on the life of an immigrant. Tears of "Yavnana" (Lullaby) immediately fill my eyes, a testament to the deep emotional connection I still hold for my homeland. The path from my home to the Great America was difficult because I left everything native. Despite the emotional struggles and the challenges, I persevered. It is also challenging to think about not knowing when I will see my children.

Stumbling is an inevitable part of the journey, but it's not the end. Like a defenseless child, you need someone to hold your hand and help you take a step properly. God made me meet many people who held my hand and helped me walk properly. They filled my soul with comfort and native warmth.

Be that as it may, an immigrant needs willpower just as a crying child needs a mother's warmth. My patience and courage have always crossed the fur bridge, a metaphor for the challenging path I've had to tread. I have fallen many times, but I have never lost my courage! I have been broken many times, but I have never cried, and so my head, left alone, rose and reached out to God.

Clinging to God, I have walked the labyrinths of my soul and America. When they ask me whether I miss my homeland, silence is the only correct answer for me. My homeland is a house built in my soul, a place that I carry with me wherever I go, a part of me that I can never leave behind. As my journey towards emigration was largely driven by the struggle for financial stability and mental growth, I remind myself daily of the importance of never losing sight of why I left home.

My heart and mind were trained to deal with difficulties from the very beginning. As I mentioned before, I did not start complaining and wailing about my homeless life. I did not complain, but what would I have achieved even if I started screaming? Therefore, I met every difficulty with my plan like a shield and took one step forward every day. I clearly explained to myself that emigration and earning money are words with different meanings, and I never confused one word with another. "Money is needed for work to be done, and work is needed, money to be earned." But the most important thing is to have a balanced attitude towards them, which protects and preserves the most precious thing: life. This balance, this perspective, was my guiding light in the darkest of times. It meant that I had to develop a good financial strategy. Whether I am a good strategist in this regard or not, I will say it out loud soon. But you know very well that spending money requires a financial plan drawn up in advance, purposefully, and that this is very important for an immigrant. The structure of financial freedom built by an immigrant can last for as few years as possible. That is why I worked on any job offered; I had to have the money to publish my books.

My teachers from Georgia, lecturers, and book editors all called me and told me they believed in me. That I could do anything also gave me strength and a responsibility not to disappoint their expectations. Wherever I studied or worked, I sowed love and friendship everywhere, understanding that this is a harvest that takes time. The Georgian reader fell in love with me and my creation, and it was what prepared my heart for great relationships. I will treasure the letter from my Georgian teacher in the ark of my life's impressions.

Khaduri Natia

Green-velvet-eyed, attractive, quite emotional schoolgirl in love with literature.

That's how I remember you, a bright and emotional student.

I'm proud to see you now, blossoming into a poet.

I'm glad that your talent split out into lines on the page; I liked your prose, poetry, self-confidence, desire for the future, feminine tenderness, and gentleness; that's all that made you able to do so much.

May your pen bless you. Entrust it to your pain and feelings; it will heal your wounds and give you the strength to overcome everything.

Your novels and poems are a joy to read, each word a testament to your talent and passion.

Your writing vision is very daring.

Poems—rather, a letter to Remarque:

"A woman must either be adored, or left..."
"Do not count the pains of a poet woman..."

As you've beautifully expressed in your work, the pains of a poet woman are not to be counted. "They bloom in her soul like a poem," each line a testament to her strength and resilience.

Or again:

"I kneeled in the graveyard of hopes,

And I presented all my soul pains to the night."

Or again:

"It was raining since the dawn...

Then a cloud appeared in my soul..."

I'm overjoyed by your accomplishments and the beauty you bring into the world through your writing.

I want to bless you on your way!

— Dali Darejan Gengiuri (Your former teacher)

My journey to becoming a writer has been a diverse one. I've worked in various fields, from finance to marketing, each offering unique experiences and insights. Yet, amidst this diversity, I always felt a pull towards the world of words and stories. It wasn't until a life-changing event, the loss of a loved one, that I fully embraced my passion for writing as a means of healing and expression.

In two years, I wrote three novels and almost a hundred poems. They are:

1) *I Forgave You.*

2) *In Jerusalem.*

3) *The Soldier's Burden.*

I called my poetry book, "And you can not tell me why I must not love you anymore!"

My main message through my writings is that we should bring more **love** and **belief** into our lives. This belief was shaped by my experiences, where I found that love and faith were the guiding lights in my darkest moments.

My belief in the transformative power of love is unshakable. I firmly hold that 'Love is the only thing you spend and multiply.' This conviction is the driving force behind my writing, infusing every word with the profound impact of love.

I write about all the feelings that create our lives and leave a profound mark on the human heart and mind. Life's leading actors are love, friendship, betrayal, faith, support, generosity, separation, forgiveness, reconciliation, and embrace.

While I always believed in the potential for success in my life, I was pleasantly surprised by the timing of my achievements. Winning an international book award soon after arriving in America was a humbling and gratifying experience that I will always cherish.

This project will always be in my heart, like my first love, and I will never forget it!

I plan to meet and collaborate with filmmakers who will make films based on my novels. My novels are based on true stories, so they will likely be very emotional films for a large audience.

I also plan to travel a lot, inspiring a lot of writing. What can stop me now when everything is already in my hands?

Today, I have to appear before an American audience. I am a little nervous, but it is neither a language barrier nor a fear of anything. It is a feeling of joy that I do not want to express and speaks to me involuntarily in my heart. Honestly, I do not even try to say anything about myself anymore. What is the need? I sometimes stop at this thought momentarily and ask my heart why I do not want to say a word about my feelings. Then, I quickly move on to the next thought to not force myself to talk about myself in a big philosophical way. Because this feeling has its actors, and I don't want to waste my energy judging myself for it, I already have much to tell and write about. How simple everything is today! After all, once, it was just a dream!

When I am in pain, my faith silences my pain, and the life that God has promised me lies ahead.

When filled with joy, I cloak my soul with the humble fabric of faith. It is not to suppress my happiness but to ensure it doesn't lead to pride or arrogance. I strive to keep my heart open and my spirit grounded, even in moments of great joy.

Talent is a gift from God, and everyone is given different talents. I was given many talents as a rare exception. For example, a mathematician cannot be a poet, and a poet cannot be a mathematician. When I worked in the financial system, I was told I was born for this job. I was told I was born for diplomacy when I enrolled in the Faculty of International Law and Relations. And this is because I always did what I did with great love. When I worked as a cleaner, I put my whole heart into my work and was the best cleaner. Tireless work and self-belief that you can and should not stop are a combination of passion, hard work, and self-belief. It's about doing what you love with all your heart, never giving up, and believing in your potential.

Along with the tears that I have shed on this path, God is not unjust not to experience the honest tears of a person and not to reward us according to the state of our hearts. Today, I stand with the mantle of happiness on my shoulders, a reward for my relentless labor and unwavering effort. This happiness, a stark contrast to the suffocating weight of pain and the relentless onslaught of suffering I once endured, is a testament to the transformative power of hard work and self-belief. It's a reminder that no matter how tough the journey, resilience can transform even the darkest moments into stepping stones towards success.

Resilience is the key to overcoming fear and exhaustion. I never knew what fatigue was. More precisely, I shouldn't have admitted my exhaustion. Otherwise, I would never have reached anything. When I was afraid, I shouldn't have noticed it either. Otherwise, I wouldn't have been able to feel the sunrise more. I had to endure everything alone! I worked day and night, physically and mentally. I started over with even greater determination if something didn't work out. I never told anyone that I was struggling spiritually. I smiled and caressed everyone. I looked after and cared for those around me. I was giving abundant love around me. It was not because I always got something in return but because I was nourished by what I gave. The measure and weight of giving love made me the person I am today, or who I am not! If I have something today, I have acquired it by showing love, and if I haven't acquired something, I have diminished it by the need to give love. Love is the purest building material of all, with which you build your personality, and day by day, you make it look like it. Yes, love has a face, and it is excellent.

Love is honest because it never gives attention to the material or immaterial things of others. Love is a worker. It works itself; it creates and builds everything in a person it wants from the beginning. Yes, betrayal and indifference cannot be the work of love. Such cold things have their own creators, who are enslaved to their works. Love, the most harmless thing ever invented, persists even in the face of betrayal. When I was betrayed, I chose to remain silent. "There is only one God whose back I have never seen because He always looks me in the eyes," I said, and I let go of the pain. It was a moment of extreme sensitivity, but I chose resilience over despair, and it was this resilience that empowered me to overcome the betrayal.

I knew this could have been a silence born out of foolishness for me, but I remained silent. What could I say?

How could you tell a person why he betrayed you?

He wanted to, and he betrayed you!

The only good thing about all this is that you will not be punished for someone else's work, and the love that lives in you will not resemble someone else's love.

Love is a profoundly personal experience unique to each individual. It's not a one-size-fits-all concept. For some, love is the solid walls of the soul, built with concrete. For others, it's a delicate mixture of dust. Each person's love is as unique as they are, and it's this uniqueness that we should always acknowledge and respect in our own experiences with love.

For some, it is a building work to be paved with one hand, and for others, walls are built on a concrete foundation while kneeling. Everyone carries their "power" with their own body, and everyone is exactly as strong as their love is capable of...

Life's challenges are the main component in the formula of love. The constant pursuit of happiness, the endurance of hardship, the battle against fear and injustice, the experience of heartache and despair, the struggle of raising children, the fight for survival, the confrontation with death, and the ability to give love are the elements that shape our capacity to love.

And finally, I will end with my favourite phrase:

"God fights together side by side with those who fight!"

NATIA KHADURI

Natia Khaduri was born in a small and amazingly beautiful country, Georgia—SAKARTVELO. She received higher education in the following specialties: mathematics, law, and international relations, and in recent years, she has been involved in the art of writing.

She is a poet and prose writer. In two years, she wrote three novels and more than a hundred poems. Now, she has moved to America and wants to further develop her creativity. Her main values are faith in God and humanity.

www.NatiaKhaduri.art
Facebook: www.facebook.com/share/1BjY4JxNZY

LEAD TO IMPACT: FROM INNER VOICE TO GLOBAL VISION

BY ROBERT G. ACOSTA

IMPACT LIFE COACH, SOCIAL ENTREPRENEUR, ATHLETE, AUTHOR OF "7 SECRETS TO HAVE IT ALL," & FOUNDER OF FULL TIME GIVER

PART I: THE STORM WITHIN

IS LIFE HAPPENING TO YOU—OR ARE YOU HAPPENING IN YOUR LIFE?

The fervid sweat was the first thing I noticed. My clothes clung to my body like I had been dragged from a Van Gogh painting—my body alive and breathless, my lungs grasping at air that wouldn't come. I opened my eyes to a blur of shapes and steam, and a sound escaped from deep within me—raw, low, unfamiliar.

I was in a room. My room. Curtains danced like geishas before an open window. The Caribbean sun spilled into space, indifferent to my dazed condition. I sat up, soaked, feet meeting the tiled floor. I peeled my clothes from my skin, wiped sweat from my brow, and stood.

That's when I saw him—outside the window. Still. Silent. Like a signpost left just for me. For one strange moment, our eyes met.

Then, just as quickly, he vanished behind a tree and a truck pulling up at the building entrance. Was he even real?

"It looks like another one bites the dust!" my wife said, entering the room before disappearing behind the bathroom door. "It's your turn to help the new neighbours with their stuff. It'll be your workout before swimming today, don't you think?"

When I started answering, the words were stuck in the middle of my throat. When I tried again, it was too late. The water running from the shower didn't allow her to hear me.

I was in one of those moments—caught in deep reflection, face-to-face with a question I couldn't ignore:

What am I really doing with my life?

Is there something I'm refusing to hear, simply because listening might demand change—or ask me to walk beside the uncomfortable companion of uncertainty?

I moved to this paradise to pause, to reset, to reflect. But most days, I still felt stuck. Living small. Shrinking.

What if this wasn't just another morning?

What if this was finally my wake-up call?

WHY IS IT WORTH IT TO STOP?

I was born and raised in Mexico City, and I learned early what success was *supposed* to look like. I had the titles, the money, the stability—and yet, deep down, I felt increasingly out of sync with myself.

In the corporate world I inhabited, advancement often meant compromising principles. If you wanted to grow, you had to play the game. Turn a blind eye. Say yes when you mean no. Smile when your soul was shaking its head.

It was subtle at first, then constant. I realized the cost of climbing higher was shrinking myself to fit into someone else's mold.

I had to stop.

But stopping—*really stopping*—feels like rebellion in a world that glorifies movement. We've been conditioned to keep going, keep producing, keep proving. But if your direction is off, speed just gets you lost faster.

Stopping is terrifying. But not stopping? That's soul-suicide.

We've all seen the films—the hero who realizes what's at stake while the rest of the world remains oblivious. They rise up, take action, and lead others. They *stand out.*

And we cheer for them. But in real life? Most people just *blend in.*

So, I had to ask myself:

What role am I playing in the story of my own life?

Because life wasn't just happening to me anymore. I had to happen *in it.*

THE LIE OF FITTING IN

Here was the problem: I was living the story I was *told* to live. A life sculpted by expectations: family, culture, society. I was choosing comfort over authenticity. Safety over truth. I buried my uniqueness in exchange for acceptance.

Acceptance was the currency, and I paid for it by denying my truth.

I call this phenomenon being in **Fitting In Mode**—the drive to belong by blending in, even if it means going numb to who you really are.

How many lies have we been told that we still believe and live our lives around?

And the moment I started questioning myself again, I remembered Robert Kiyosaki's quote: "It's not what you say out of your mouth that determines your life. It is what you whisper to yourself that has the most power."

Fitting in was no longer an option. I knew I had to **stand out**.

It was time to flip the script.

It began with a single shift—from **outside-in** living to **inside-out** living.

The opposite of Fitting In isn't rebellion. It's **Standing Out.**

And standing out doesn't mean shouting or dominating—it means living **Inside-Out**. It means having the courage to follow your intuition, even when it scares you. Especially when it scares you.

Living Inside-Out—that is, not reacting to life, but consciously shaping it from within—shouldn't be difficult.

But we've been trained—no, conditioned for centuries—to avoid it. Because of that conditioning, living Inside-Out today feels hard. It's lonely. Unpopular. Misjudged or misunderstood by the average person. It's wildly emotional. And deeply, profoundly personal.

Sadly, the bad news doesn't stop there.

Choosing to live this way goes directly against two powerful forces that govern our lives:

The first is our **social upbringing—to fit in.**

The second is **our biological wiring—to stay safe.**

And that was my challenge.

My battle wasn't with the world. It wasn't with others. It was 100% internal. The battle was against myself.

This was my inner war. A battle against the part of me that—socially and biologically—preferred comfort over calling.

While I was lost in thought, a quieter voice rose from within—this time from an anonymous author, **"When it comes to your dreams, you have two choices: pursue them or be haunted by them."**

There was nothing left to question—I had made my decision. It was time to **Stand Out.** To lead my life. To shape it from the inside out.

It's not easy. It's *never* easy. But it's necessary.

And it demands something radical: **Leadership.**

UNCOVERING THE LEADER WITHIN

Ironically, I had been practicing leadership long before I ever gave it a name.

I can still picture it vividly, as if it were yesterday—that corner of the building that always caught the most sunlight at that particular time of afternoon. No wonder it was the CEO's favourite spot to discuss innovative ideas with his team—and with the not always welcome Market Research department.

As part of that department, my job required a high tolerance for ambivalence. One day, they'd praise you for backing up their bold ideas with statistically sound consumer insights. The next, you'd catch sideways glances when those same insights forced them back to the drawing board—after being told their concept "wouldn't fly."

For more than thirty years, I carried out key responsibilities in my professional life—many of them unconsciously—that reflected the essence of true leadership.

It's not easy to stand in front of a CEO and tell them their idea isn't as strong as they believe. In fact, most avoid that situation entirely, out of fear of "retaliation."

So, I was that guy—the one who dared to challenge the board of directors when data revealed an uncomfortable truth. I wasn't trying to rebel. I was trying to **protect the vision**. Because deep down, I believed in it. I saw where the company could go, and I wasn't afraid to say what needed to be said to get us there.

Could this have been a form of leadership—a quiet, subtle kind that worked behind the scenes?

Whatever it was, it planted a seed. And without a doubt, it prepared me for what was coming.

MEETING MY FUTURE SELF

NOW, the "new me"—at least in my mind—the "me" convinced that to interrupt the autopilot story of my life, I had to stand out rather than keep trying to fit in, knew one thing: I must lead my own vision to become…

To become what, exactly?

What kind of leader do I need to become?

Not again! Just when I thought I had the answer, more questions rose from the silence—persistent, insistent, as if daring me to grow beyond what I thought I knew.

This time, I knew I couldn't resist. I had to accept that the questions —the enigmas—were part of the path.

And in the stillness of one restless night, when the mind quieted, and the soul spoke, something came to me—not noise, not thought, but a revelation… in disguise. Clues, perhaps. Not the final answer, but enough to keep going. Enough to know I was getting closer.

I wasn't sure if the blur before my eyes was proof enough that I was dreaming, but the water still clouded my vision as I barely made out the silhouette of someone in the distance.

Shaking my head, I could now see a man standing beside the chair where I had clumsily placed my swimming bag. A few steps more, and I saw him staring at me—then at the sand between us, as if paving a path with his eyes and drawing me toward him until I stood just a few feet away.

"You're a skilled swimmer," the man said, his voice peculiar—like it had echoed out of a dark cave.

"Trying to be," I replied, a shy smile tugging at my face.

"You don't exactly look like the swimmer type, though," I added, eyeing his long but thin raincoat, which concealed most of his body.

Right after speaking, I realized I'd been a bit rude to a complete stranger. Still, the fact that he was so close to my things made me uneasy. I tend to get instinctively defensive when it comes to matters of priority—especially my swimming routine.

"Not my sport lately," he replied. "But I can tell it suits you well."

I was still holding my towel over my head as he gave me a noticeable glance, scanning my lean, athletic frame.

My mind drifted back to my early days of swimming.

An outdoor semi-Olympic pool had witnessed my transformation into a skilled child swimmer. I couldn't remember much about the training itself, but I had vivid memories of medals, cheers, and the proud faces of my parents and relatives watching from the windows.

I grew up in a supportive environment, living a by-the-book life. But something inside me began to stir after I graduated from university— something I couldn't yet define, though I could feel it growing.

We all seek—or at least long for—a revelation. A moment of clarity to show us the path: the brilliant, effortless path that fulfills our desires and lets us walk confidently, harvesting better results day by day.

How many nights do we spend wondering how life could be… if only? Then comes the silence. The echo. The emptiness that feels like it may never be filled. Weeks, months, even years may pass without answers—or without the ability to recognize them.

Was it here just a moment ago, and I missed it? Was it so well disguised that I assumed it wasn't meant for me?

Whatever form it takes, it comes. At some point in our lives, it arrives.

Back to the dream… Curiosity tugged at me.

"Is there any particular reason you were waiting for me—right now, right here?" I asked, trying this time to sound less blunt.

Without a word, the man pulled a photograph from his jacket and held it inches from my face. The shadows were quickly overtaking the last light of day. The photo showed several people posing casually.

As he asked whether I recognized anyone in it, I instinctively pulled away, reclaiming my personal space.

"I don't need to answer anything," I snapped. "Who are you? Why are you here? What do you want?"

My words came out like a sudden wave—rhetorical, breathless, borderline defensive. The photo slipped from his hand and landed on the dark sand beneath the chair. I caught a glimpse of one face that immediately grabbed my attention. The man didn't move. Not a blink. He didn't even glance at the photo.

"It's not for me to say," he replied. "But I do believe you could answer my question first."

His voice somehow reached me without his face changing—his lips barely parting as the words escaped into the thickening night.

Frustrated, I scooped up my things—towel, goggles, swim cap—clutching them in my arms as I turned and walked away.

I didn't speak. Just stomped down the sand with long, deliberate strides, scattering grains like heavy raindrops bursting around my feet.

Darkness had fully arrived, claiming the atmosphere with finality—welcoming the last breaths of one day and the first of the next.

I knew this moment was meant to be. The night was settled.

So was I.

I was determined to erase the image from my mind—the one I'd just seen in that photograph. I don't anger easily. But when questioned unexpectedly—especially by a stranger—I can become reactive. It's a tendency shaped by years in over-analytical, high-stakes environments. An art form I mastered in silence, hidden behind professionalism and instinct.

A few months after that dream—after receiving that "message"—the mystery remained unresolved. Until it finally clicked: the man in the picture was me. But there was more to it than that.

There was something in his eyes: **Certainty. Strength. Peace.**

It wasn't who I was. And it wasn't who I had been. It was who I was *becoming.* That man—my future self—was the vision.

And I realized: I don't just have to achieve something.

I have to BECOME someone.

That's the real calling of leadership.

PART II: THE UNFOLDING OF A LEADER

WHEN EFFORT & COURAGE AREN'T ENOUGH

The dream stayed with me—haunting, illuminating. The man in the raincoat had shown me something I couldn't unsee: **a vision of who I was destined to become.**

Not a fantasy, not a hope. A **future-self** calling me forward.

But how do you become the person you were meant to be? That question echoed louder than all the noise around me. Because now, the "new me"—the man determined to stop fitting in and finally **stand out**—understood something vital:

"Effort and courage are not enough without purpose and direction."
~ John F. Kennedy

I had been working hard. I had been brave. But I was still unclear on **where** to aim it all.

I needed to lead, yes—but lead *toward what*?

And then came the deeper realization: To lead others, **I first had to lead myself. Leadership was already in me.**

That's when my past began making sense.

Back in my corporate life, I had often been the quiet voice of reason, the bridge between data and decision. I didn't call it leadership then. I was just doing what felt right—defending the truth, protecting the vision, anchoring the future.

I wasn't loud. I wasn't flashy. But I was dependable. People came to me because they knew I'd speak honestly—even when it wasn't easy.

That's leadership. It had been there all along. Unconscious. Subtle. **Unclaimed.**

But now? I had to own it. Because the path ahead required *conscious leadership*—intentional, visionary, and bold.

And I needed to test it. To challenge myself. To stretch beyond the limits I had accepted for too long.

STANDING OUT: FOR REAL THIS TIME

So, I made a decision: I would use one of my favourite skills—swimming—to go from the island of Cancun to the island of Isla Mujeres.

A little over six miles between the two islands. A physical challenge, yes—but far more than that, it was symbolic. It was the embodiment of standing out, of setting a personal standard, of **choosing to live in a state of success** before any medal ever touched my neck.

I trained relentlessly. Early mornings. Clean eating. Discipline. Focus. Sacrifice.

But something strange began to happen along the way. I started *becoming* the man in the photograph—not because I would complete the swim, but because I had committed to **becoming someone capable of it.** That shift changed everything.

When race day arrived, I didn't just show up to compete. I showed up already victorious. I was already living in the *state* I had once only imagined.

Two hours and twenty minutes later, I stood at the shore of Isla Mujeres, under the burning sun, endless drops of salty water clinging to my body, a medal on my neck. I wasn't gasping for breath—I was breathing deeper than I had in years.

That swim was never about distance. It was about becoming. It was about leading myself through the unknown. And it was the turning point.

CHOOSING THE STATE OF SUCCESS

Here's the secret: Success isn't a destination. It's a *state of being* you choose to live in now.

You don't wait for the result to feel accomplished. You *embody* it in every step, every breath, every decision—until the outside catches up.

This realization unlocked something foundational in me: The first principle of *exceptional leadership* is to lead from the **inside out**—with integrity, purpose, and unshakable belief in the vision.

But more importantly… *It's not about you.*

YOUR LIFE IS NOT ABOUT YOU

We all want to grow. To evolve. To be free. To create. But if the outcome only benefits *you*, it will never fulfill you.

True fulfillment comes when your success spills over—when it becomes a gift, a ripple, a contribution. That's the mark of a leader.

That's when I saw it clearly: My mission wasn't to succeed for myself. It was to succeed so I could *serve others.*

And to serve well, I had to stop being a lone wolf. I had to stop climbing for personal gain. I had to start **investing in people**—raising others to become leaders too.

Because one leader alone can spark change. But many leaders together can **reshape the world.**

PART III: FROM IMPACT TO LEGACY

THIS ISN'T ABOUT ME

Once you realize your life is not about you, everything changes.

The weight of performance. The obsession with recognition. The need to prove something to someone—it all falls away.

You stop striving. You start serving.

And from that place, leadership is no longer about *being in charge.* It becomes about *creating change.*

What I discovered was this: **If you want to make a real, lasting difference—lead others.**

Because impact without people is impossible. Because a legacy without leaders is short-lived.

I had spent years searching for significance, never realizing it was right in front of me… in the lives I had already touched. The stories people shared. The quiet thank yous. The moments when something I said or did made someone stand taller, believe deeper, act bolder.

That's when it hit me:

My real purpose is not just to live my vision. It's to multiply it through others.

LEADERSHIP REIMAGINED

The world doesn't need more bosses, authorities, or lone saviours. What we need is a new kind of leader, one not defined by power or position, but by:

Vision grounded in reality and hope.

Courage to move forward without guarantees.

Humility to listen, adapt, and walk with others.

Resilience to fail and keep going.

Collaboration as the default, not the exception.

I call this **Humanae Leadership.**

It's the kind of leadership that recognizes our shared humanity. That sees leadership not as domination, but as *activation*. Not a title, not a position, but a mindset. Not about being followed, but about *raising* others to lead.

A way of showing up in the world—with vision, purpose, and the will to serve something greater than yourself. It's what I had been becoming all along. Now, it was time to give it away.

THE CRISIS & THE CALL

We live in a world on the edge. Technological disruption, political division, climate emergencies, and spiritual confusion.

But as Tony Seba and James Arbib remind us:

"Dark ages do not occur for lack of sunshine,

but for lack of leadership."

We have the tools. We have the knowledge. We even have the foresight.

What we need now is a **generation bold enough to lead—not because they were chosen, but because they** *chose themselves.*

"Choice, not chance, determines your destiny."
~ Aristotle

That's what this moment is about.

You're not reading this by accident. You're here because you *sense* it, too. The call. The fire. The whisper that says: *"It's your time."*

THE HUMANAE LEADERS MANIFESTO

Let me leave you with the foundation that guides this new generation:

What we aim for is not a single purpose—each leader must discover their own. **What we achieve** is not merely material—but rich, abundant, and meaningful. **What we pursue** is not a lone hero's quest—but a collaborative, human journey. **What we do** is not about saving the planet—but learning to be better guests. **How we live** is not always easy or happy—but we choose to savour every second. **What we hope for** is not just for me or you today—but for generations yet to come.

A FINAL WORD

If you've read this far, perhaps a voice inside of you is stirring—the same voice that once spoke to me, that still does.

It may not sound like thunder. It may be no louder than a whisper. But it's there.

You are not here to play small. You are not here to just fit in.

You are here to **lead.**

To **serve.**

To **impact.**

You are here to raise your banner, even if no one else has yet. You are here to become the leader you've been waiting for.

Now it's your turn. The world needs you.

Lead to Impact.

ROBERT G. ACOSTA

Robert Acosta is an Impact Life Coach, social entrepreneur, and athlete who helps business professionals, entrepreneurs, consultants, and growth-driven individuals achieve personal alignment, financial success, and a clear path to building a lasting legacy.

His dedication to holistic wellness—mental, physical, and financial —shows through in his work, empowering others to design a self-directed, meaningful, and impactful Big Life.

Originally from Mexico City and now based in Toronto, Canada, Robert brings a unique blend of analytical insight and passion for human potential. With a background in actuarial sciences and a specialization in consumer and human behaviour, he has spent three decades working with leading international brands, shaping strategies that drive innovation, growth, and transformation.

For Robert, leadership is not a title or a position—it is a response to an inner call to live with alignment, meaning, and impact.

What is your inner voice telling you?

Are you hearing the call of leadership—not louder motivation, but deeper alignment?

If this resonates, I invite you to continue the conversation.

www.linkedin.com/in/RobertGAcosta
TikTok: @RobertG_Acosta

DON'T GET DERAILED: FINDING CLARITY IN CHAOS

BY SHERREE' BOWEN

INTERNATIONAL AWARD-WINNING CHRISTIAN AUTHOR & THOUGHT-LEADER, WOMEN'S ENRICHMENT SPEAKER & GROUP LEADERSHIP COACH, & AWARD-WINNING CHRISTIAN VOCALIST

Have you ever put on a smile while feeling like you're about to break inside? I understand that feeling all too well. I spent years standing on stages, singing and speaking—doing the one thing I felt I was born to do. In those moments, I could focus. The weight of my struggles temporarily lifted as I connected with the audience. Their smiles, their genuine interest—it felt like they saw me, perhaps even loved me more than I loved myself. These interactions gave me a sense of peace, even if only for a few days. But the moment I stepped off that stage, reality hit. The peace faded, and I was left wondering, *What now?*

Like many, I faced hardships that tested my sense of purpose. My ministry was my passion, yet I struggled to make all the pieces fit. I kept questioning my direction—*Was I meant to do more? Had I chosen the right path?* Singing and speaking came naturally, but the uncertainty of what lay beyond the stage left me feeling lost. Without that outlet, I wrestled with doubt, making choices I later regretted. In my search for meaning, I took detours—some that cost me time, relationships, and made me question my self-worth.

At some point, I had to face a difficult truth: **my past mistakes did not define me, but my mindset about them did.** Instead of viewing myself through the lens of regret, I had to learn to extract lessons from my experiences. **Self-worth isn't measured by perfect choices but by resilience, learning, and growth.**

So, I ask you: *How can you shift your perspective on past decisions to ensure they don't dictate your future? How can you realign with your goals and become the best version of yourself?*

The answer lies in intention. Success doesn't happen by accident; it starts with a clear question of "why." When we move with intention, our actions align with our purpose. If I were to ask you what drives you—what truly fuels your ambition—what would you say? Would it be the fear of failure or the drive to be more than where you came from? What would truly be your driving force for success?

Your answer cannot simply be "my family" or "financial stability." While those are important, we need to dig deeper. What is the force that compels you to wake up every morning and push forward, even when life gets tough? **Without a clear vision, it's easy to get stuck in cycles of frustration, blame, and stagnation.**

Instead of dwelling on what's missing, focus on what's possible. Instead of wishing for a piece of success, learn the entire process— and own it. No one is coming to save you. At the end of the day, no one can love you, advocate for you, or fight for your dreams the way you can. **Your breakthrough begins when you decide to take responsibility for your own growth.**

THE POWER OF PERSPECTIVE: CLAIMING YOUR SUCCESS

Ask yourself this: How can I shift my perspective on past choices to ensure I never repeat the same mistakes? How can I become the best version of the person I dream of being? Trust me, there are answers to these questions. You ask how I know? Because I have questioned myself many times while figuring out my plan. We all, no matter our level of success, have stumbled while planning our growth strategy. Every new day we are given, our plans get adjusted by circumstances. Don't let failures or unexpected outcomes define your goals. Stay the path—everyone faces challenges, but consider them a chance to increase and grow.

One of the greatest lessons I've learned is that **success starts with intention**. No one achieves greatness by accident. Every accomplishment begins with a clear reason—a powerful 'why' that fuels your determination. Every achievement has a driving force behind its motivation. You can't win the game without a strong goal and a plan.

You have to find that "IT" factor, that one thing that makes you think, this is my direction, this is what I have been praying for. Discernment has a huge impact when you take the time to "be still" and listen.

- We all have an assignment—a God-given plan. So, what will you do with your life assignment? How can you utilize your gifts, talents, and knowledge?

Have you considered exactly what internal fire motivates you? The thing that compels you to keep going even when things get tough?

You can't win in life if you don't have a clear goal and a plan. Success doesn't come from external circumstances—it starts within you. You have to take accountability. Look in the mirror and be honest with yourself:

It's *ME* who isn't putting in the work.

It's *ME* who isn't making the time.

It's *ME* who keeps making excuses.

Complaining about what you don't have or how hard life has been will never move you forward. Instead of focusing on what's missing, shift your focus to what's possible.

Instead of asking for a "piece" of the pie, learn the entire recipe. This is what I learned from my setbacks—change will not happen until you take responsibility for it. No one is coming to fix your situation for you. push through, and fight for your dreams, you are your own biggest advocate!

I've met so many people who say, "I'm not qualified for this" or "I don't think I'm good enough to lead." But let me tell you this: it's not about being "ready"—it's about being willing. When you say YES to your dreams, when you step forward in faith, God will equip you with everything you need—things you never even thought were possible.

So, let's break it down:

You must make a choice!

You must *decide to move forward*, even when you feel uncertain.

You must *be intentional* about stepping into the next level of your life.

The only way to rise to the next stage of your success—your growth, your breakthrough—is to commit to yourself first. It starts with a single decision: Are you willing to take ownership of your future?

BREAKING FREE FROM STAGNATION: OWNING YOUR PATH TO GROWTH

If you don't take action, you'll find yourself sitting in the same old recliner, eating popcorn, watching the same movie of your life play out—knowing exactly how it ends. Same job, same desk, same routine. Feeling burned out while your circle of friends pats you on the back, saying, "You're doing great!"—when deep down, you know you're not. They encourage you to "Do you" because, to them, your life seems fine just the way it is. But here's the truth: staying where you are just because it's comfortable is a trap.

Even well-meaning people may not push you to grow, because they're comfortable with who you are today. But no one is going to look out for your success the way you will. You've probably heard the saying: You are the average of the five people you spend the most time with. If you surround yourself with people who lack vision, people who are content with mediocrity, guess what? That mindset will rub off on you.

So, ask yourself:

Am I where I truly want to be?

Is this the legacy I want to leave behind?

Or do I want more?

Let me tell you from a faith perspective.

All you have to do is say the word "*YES,*" and you will find that God will equip you with the things you never thought were possible. You have a choice in deciding your next endeavor, your next move, and your next increase. The way to get there is to find the faith within yourself and believe that you can do all things through Christ. He gives the strength to make your goals attainable.

Most of us don't want to remain stagnant—we want to grow, evolve, and become better versions of ourselves. Staying the same, never challenging yourself, is not only boring—it's a slow way of fading into irrelevance. The good news? Success has no age limit. Whether you're in your 20s, 30s, 50s, or beyond, your next level starts with you.

THE POWER OF LEGACY & PURPOSE

We all hit walls—moments of brokenness, feelings of being less than. But let me remind you of something important: God used the broken. He didn't call the smartest, the most talented, or the most polished. He called those who were willing. He gave assignments to people who had a hunger for more, those who were willing to step forward and take action despite their circumstances.

You have an assignment. And that assignment is not to sit back and reminisce about who you used to be or what you once achieved. It is to step fully into the person you were designed to become. Your legacy matters.

Too often, we overlook the power of legacy. My father was a pastor, and for years, I listened to him preach powerful messages. They were uplifting, inspiring. But, like many of us, I'd leave those services thinking, Wow, that was amazing! I need to apply that to my life!— only to let Monday roll around, and nothing changed.

How often do we do that? We attend an event, hear a powerful message, and feel on fire with motivation—only to let the excitement fade once real life kicks in. Transformation only happens when we take what we've learned and apply it consistently. I realize that we often take pause to find clarity and balance. But let's not forget that just as Simon Peter cast his net for hours, even into the next day, and then, in frustration, told Jesus (in my words), "Look, I have been fishing throughout the night, and there is nothing to be found."

Jesus said, "Go back out, into the deep waters, cast your net on the right side of the boat, and watch what happens." So they did, even with hesitation, and sure enough, there were so many fish the boat wouldn't hold them. 153 to be exact. I can only imagine his frustration and hesitation to try again.

Isn't that the way we are today? We try something, fail, then say, "Well, that will never work." I've already tried it, so I'm not going to waste anymore of my time.

I say to you—don't doubt yourself, just as Simon Peter did, cast your net even if you feel it isn't going to be enough, the KEY is to have FAITH, then believe in your ability to achieve anything you set your mind to. That will be when you'll experience just how life can change, But It has to begin with YOU! Are you willing?

APPRECIATE WHAT YOU HAVE BEFORE IT'S GONE

When I lost my father to a stroke, followed by my mother a little over a year later, my perspective on life shifted drastically. The lessons they taught me—the wisdom they shared—became crystal clear in their absence. I had unintentionally taken their words for granted, dismissing them as part of everyday life. It wasn't until they were gone that I truly saw the depth of the legacy they

left behind. I'll stop here and ask you- If you had to write down your accomplishments, what would that look like? If YOU'RE not satisfied with how that would read, then now is the time to start building your legacy, the one you would be proud of.

Don't wait until it's too late to appreciate the wisdom, opportunities, and gifts in front of you. Don't waste your years simply existing— build something meaningful, prepare for your future, and pursue the success you were meant for.

At the end of the day, the only person who can stop you from achieving your dreams is YOU. So, ask yourself:

What do you want your legacy to say about you?

If you haven't yet discovered your purpose, now is the time. You are more than your past mistakes, more than your last bad decision. Success starts with clarity—knowing what you want and writing it down. In fact, the Bible emphasizes this principle in Habakkuk 2:2: "Write the vision and make it plain upon tables." Your vision should be a daily reminder, something you reflect on every morning.

But here's the key: No more excuses. Stop blaming your past, your circumstances, or the people who didn't support you. Your success is in your hands. It's time to take ownership of your future.

Speak life over yourself. Use affirmations like:

* *I am capable.*

* *I am smart enough.*

* *I am blessed and worthy of success.*

I have the talent and ambition to achieve my dreams. We have been designed for such a time as this. So, If *HE* said it, then we should believe it!

Your thoughts shape your reality, so start focusing on where you ARE going, not where you have been. Design your vision for success, then step forward and claim that plan for your life. The Bible reminds us in Matthew 7:7: "Ask and it will be given to you; seek, and you will find; knock and the door will be opened."

If you truly desire something, you must act on it and have faith that you WILL complete your goal! The driving force for success is one word: **YOU.**

* YOU - *Submit*

* YOU - Make the plan

* YOU - Claim it over your life

* YOU - Give it to God

* YOU - Is where life begins

Your life's purpose cannot happen without a "You" plan!

THE REALITY OF OBSTACLES:
A LESSON IN PERSEVERANCE

Let me share the story of my husband, John—a natural athlete. He played multiple sports in high school and pursued his dream of playing football while working full-time and studying to become a pharmacist. He had no financial safety net, but he was determined to make it on his own.

His schedule was relentless, balancing work, training, and school. He had his sights set on playing for the University of Tennessee as a walk-on. But life had other plans.

As semesters piled up, he had to transfer to a smaller college to finish his degree. Still, he didn't let go of his dream. He trained harder than ever, eventually earning two opportunities to try out for the NFL Combine—first with the Atlanta Falcons, then with the Oakland Raiders.

The second tryout was his moment. He had trained for this, sacrificed for this. He sprinted down the field, clocking an impressive 4.32-second run. But then, he was cut by a tenth of a second. His dream slipped away in an instant.

John could have let that failure define him. Instead, he shifted his mindset. He stopped focusing on what didn't happen and started looking at what he had gained: discipline, resilience, and an unstoppable drive that would fuel his next endeavor.

TURN SETBACKS INTO SETUPS FOR SUCCESS

We all know what it's like to give something our all, only to fall short. But setbacks are not roadblocks—they are redirections. Every time you face a disappointment, you have two choices:

Let it define you and stop moving forward.

Use it as fuel to pivot and push toward something even greater.

Your next opportunity may be better than the one you thought you lost. But you'll never know if you stop now.

Instead of dwelling on failure, ask yourself:

What did I learn from this experience?

How can I use this lesson to grow?

What new doors are opening because of this setback?

You have everything you need to succeed. Don't waste time wishing—start moving. Your greatest breakthrough is on the other side of your perseverance.

We still have John's jersey and combine T-shirts as a reminder that some goals in life are not final destinations but directional stepping stones. Often, we believe that one specific path is the only way to success, but sometimes, God has a different plan—one that we don't yet understand.

One of my favorite scriptures, Jeremiah 29:11, reminds us of this truth: "For I know the plans I have for you, declares the Lord, plans to prosper you and not to harm you, plans to give you hope and a future." No matter the disappointments we face, we can trust that we are being led toward something greater.

But let's be clear: faith without action is fruitless. As 2 Thessalonians 3:10 reminds us, "If anyone will not work, neither shall he eat." Success requires effort, persistence, and the discipline to move forward. Sitting still and waiting for things to change will never lead to progress.

PROCRASTINATION IS SIMPLY THE
SILENT THIEF OF SUCCESS

Too many people let procrastination rob them of their dreams. At its core, procrastination involves you choosing to do something less urgent and more enjoyable over the task that needs immediate attention.

See, this isn't just about poor time management; it's a complex interplay of psychological factors.

* *Fear of failure*

* *Perfectionism*

* *And even the thrill of last-minute pressure*

Procrastination is a pervasive issue that can significantly impact your future. By understanding the root cause of your situation and implementing a strong strategy to overcome it, you can reduce the hold procrastination has over your life. As with many behavioral issues, **perseverance and patience are key to overcoming procrastination.**

We tell ourselves, "I'll do it tomorrow," but tomorrow never comes. Days turn into weeks, weeks into months, and before we know it, we're still in the same place, making the same excuses.

Success doesn't wait for perfect timing. It requires taking action now. Ask yourself: What lessons can I apply from my past struggles? What habits do I need to break to move forward? What's stopping me from taking action today?

Excuses are the enemy of progress. If your dreams were on fire, would you wait until later to put them out? No! You'd act immediately. Apply that same urgency to your goals.

CHANGE YOUR CIRCLE, CHANGE YOUR FUTURE

Growth requires change. If you're always surrounded by people who think small, play it safe, and accept mediocrity, guess what? You'll become just like them. Who you surround yourself with shapes your future.

If you want to level up, ask yourself:

Are the people around me helping me grow?

Am I surrounding myself with visionaries or complainers? Do my relationships challenge me to become better?

Seasons change when we do: *If you want different results, it's time to make different choices.*

So, what's holding you back? It's time to stop circling the same mountain of excuses and step boldly toward the future you were meant to live. Write down your insecurities, face them, and take action.

Your next breakthrough is waiting on the other side of your decision to move forward.

After reflecting on those questions, were your answers surprising? Or did you already know the obstacles holding you back? Either way, it doesn't matter. What matters is what you do next. Today is your day to say, "I am going to win," and take real, intentional action toward your future.

I had to go through this exact process. I know what it feels like to be lost, to feel as if life has spiraled out of control. I made mistakes, took wrong turns, and spent years trying to piece things back together. But one day, I woke up and made a choice—I refused to be defined by my past. I stood in front of the mirror and declared, "This is not who I am, and this is not the life God intended for me." That moment changed everything.

I surrendered my fears, my doubts, and my regrets. I put my faith in God and took action. I wrote down my vision, realigned my purpose, and doors began to open. No, the struggles didn't magically disappear, but my mindset shifted. I realized that every challenge was an opportunity to learn, to grow, and to step into a stronger version of myself. **Your transformation starts when you stop waiting and start moving.**

If you fail, remember: Having an imperfect plan today is better than waiting for the perfect one that never happens. Just start! Adjust as you go. The greatest lessons come from the journey itself. You won't always have the answers at the beginning, but you'll figure them out along the way.

If you're thinking, I'm not a leader. I don't have the skills to succeed —let me tell you this: leadership is not about standing on a stage or holding a title. Leadership is about taking charge of your own life. It's about deciding that your future is worth fighting for. It's about being an example to those around you, whether you realize it or not. Someone is watching how you rise from your struggles, and your story will inspire them to do the same.

I always tell my kids, "Without valleys, we would never appreciate the beauty of the mountaintop." Every setback, every misstep, every challenge you face is teaching you something valuable. The key is to keep moving, keep learning, and keep your eyes on your personal vision ahead.

Success is not accidental. Within the realm of critical theology, success is built with the intention of having a focused commitment to living out our lives with faith.

Spiritual endeavors encourage us as individuals to engage within ourselves, and applying this principle ensures us that our Journey is purposeful and fulfilling.

By applying this mindset, you will achieve your desired goals and put yourself on the path towards a higher quality of success and lifestyle.

Stay focused, stay committed, and don't let anything—not fear, not doubt, not failure—derail you from the destiny that is waiting for you. This is your time. Step forward and claim it.

God's not done with you! *So, let's get busy.*

226

SHERREE' BOWEN

Sherree' Bowen is an award-winning author, speaker, and ministry leader dedicated to empowering women through faith-based teaching, transformational events, and authentic conversations that foster spiritual growth and purpose-driven living. She is the founder of SB Ministries Inc., where she leads women's conferences, leadership events, and teaching-coaching masterminds across the United States.

Her breakout book, *When Life Gets Messy, Make It Your Ministry*, published with TBN Trilogy Christian Publishing, turns real-life chaos into Kingdom purpose. Sherree' is a signed author with TBN Trilogy, and her work is widely used in women's small groups and ministry settings.

Sherree' holds a Ph.D. in Philosophy in Christian Education with a concentration in Ministry Leadership. Known for her fun, faith-filled, and practical teaching style, she lights up rooms with messages that leave audiences laughing, learning, and leaning deeper into Jesus.

www.SherreeBowen.com
Instagram: *@sherreebowen18*

A LIFE WORTH LIVING: EVALUATING YOUR ACTIONS TO CULTIVATE A LIFE OF PURPOSE AND IMPACT

BY SPENCE TRICK

CO-OWNER OF WAKESURF TAMPA, FOUNDER OF THE WAKESPORTS CLUB AT THE UNIVERSITY OF ALABAMA, & CHRISTIAN LEADER

HOW I STUMBLED MY WAY INTO IMPACT

Have you ever had a moment in your life where the reality that you were walking in didn't match the expectations that you had set for it?

Well, I can confidently say I have.

Very few people can say they are working their dream job. I was blessed to be one of those very few. Not only that, but I had stepped into this role as soon as I had graduated from college. It was truly picture-perfect, like something you'd see in a movie. Little did I know, I would soon find out that it wasn't going to be everything I had thought it would be.

As a fresh college graduate from the University of Alabama, I moved to Tampa, Florida, to run a watersports charter company. Since I started the Wakesports Club at The University of Alabama while in college, I thought this job would be the perfect fit for me, combining my passion with my expertise. I mean, after all, who wouldn't want to move to Florida after graduation to literally live on the water? Not only would I be able to be on the water frequently doing what I loved, but I would be able to develop my business skills and become a more experienced business leader.

Those were just the perks on paper, but as an added bonus, I was also getting the freedom to live whatever kind of life I wanted, now that I was fully able to fund myself. This can be incredibly freeing and fulfilling, or it can be immeasurably restricting and draining. What's interesting is the paradoxical nature of it. I chose what I thought was the free route, which meant going out to expensive dinners, going to the clubs, inviting plenty of random women on the boat on our free days, and many other seemingly extravagant experiences.

While this experience may have seemed like clips straight out of The Wolf of Wall Street, it also left me just as empty and broken as Jordan Belfort when he lost everything. That's right, the freedom that I was so diligently seeking in my own pleasure turned out to be a trap. I was stuck in the same cycles each week, looking to get my next fill. Yet nothing I sought after truly filled me.

In a lifestyle defined by complete freedom and happiness as the world defines it, I was left with no purpose, no sense of fulfillment, and no peace. In addition, I couldn't see any real value in my life, as I had no impact on those around me. I mean, how could I, when I was chasing the wrong things myself? I thought there had to be more to running a business, more to relationships, and more to life, for that matter. I craved meaningful work, relationships, and impact. I craved a life of significance. But I had no idea what that looked like, or how to achieve it.

Six months went by, and nothing changed. It was the same thing over and over. Cycles of temporary pleasure and excitement, followed by a deep sense of discontentment and longing for more.

Then I moved about thirty minutes away to Clearwater, Florida, to simplify logistics for my business. Looking back, I realize this was a pivotal moment in my life. After moving, I vividly remember feeling the need to get connected to a church. I didn't connect the dots that this might be the void in my life that I had been trying to fill with everything else. And that's when I found Radiant.

I stumbled into this church held in a high school one Sunday morning. And that was the Sunday that marked the beginning of my life transformation—the start down a long path to a life of true impact.

I was seeking genuine connection and deeper relationships, so I decided to start serving at church on Sundays. Little did I know that this would be the avenue that introduced me to my now best friend. Not only that, but this friend would also invite me to join one of his small groups, which would change my life forever. It was in a living room full of ten men at the first meeting of this small group that I first learned the impact that one story can have.

We are all created uniquely, with experiences that shape the person we become. These experiences become our story. Our stories have power. In fact, they have the power to change other people's lives. I've heard it said that people only change in two states: inspiration and desperation. Stories have the power to reveal one's own desperation by relating to another's circumstances. They also have the power to highlight one person's desperation in a way that can turn it into another person's inspiration. This is precisely what happened to me. One man's story of desperation would inspire me to make a shift in my life, never to look back again.

This story helped me realize that I wasn't at rock bottom, but that I could get there very easily if I wasn't careful. So, I began making intentional changes in my life to set a new trajectory for my future.
Now, almost two years later, I can confidently say that I know what I was missing during that time of my life. It was a relationship with God. I finally understood why I lacked purpose and fulfillment. I was chasing everything and everyone, except the only One who could

give me what I was looking for. I understand why I had no peace. I had no foundation, so I was getting rocked by the waves and the wind of life. I had nothing to believe in, nothing to hope for, and no sense of truth. It was then that I realized that without a purpose and a vision accompanying it, we wander aimlessly through life.

Now that I recognized what I was missing and began taking steps, I began to experience the peace, joy, and fulfillment I had been so desperately longing for. Not only that, but my life began to bear fruit and have a far more lasting impact on those around me. I began to hear stories of how other people's lives were changed because of a group I led, a conversation I'd had, or something I'd been a part of.

But it wasn't easy. I had to stop doing some things I thought I wanted to do. I had to quit hanging out with some of the people I thought I wanted to hang out with. I had to deny myself and some of my greatest desires. Only then was I able to see fruit in my life. The interesting thing I learned about the value of discipline and sacrifice is that discipline breeds desire. This is a powerful tool: you can leverage a discipline to cultivate a healthy desire, allowing you to sustain healthy habits.

If we're not careful, we can easily walk through the hustle and bustle of life and miss out on the opportunities placed before us to be a leader who leaves a lasting impact. It takes us slowing down and being intentional to truly lead a life of lasting impact. It takes consistency. It takes a belief in yourself that you do have a calling and a purpose. Looking back, I'm so grateful I took that leap of faith in my life. I think about how my life could've been so insignificant had I not stepped into the discomfort that was the unknown in front of me.

So, now I ask you, is there anything holding you back from becoming the impact leader that you were created to be? Is there anything in your life that you need to get rid of, stop doing, or stop thinking about to walk into your purpose? Or maybe you're wondering, what does it even mean to *actually* leave an impact?

Let's dissect this so you can be a leader who leaves a meaningful impact.

WHAT DOES IT MEAN TO BE AN
IMPACT LEADER TO YOU?

Do you want to make a difference with your life? I'm willing to bet that you want your legacy to be something significant. I consider this the very mindset of an impact leader. Before we go any further, I think it's important that we define the two words: impact and leader.

Impact: the force of impression of one thing on another: a significant or major effect

Leader: a person who has commanding authority or influence

By the definitions of these words, we can see that an impact leader is someone of influence who has a significant effect on something or someone. This is pretty open-ended, but it allows you to see how you can be an impactful leader in your respective profession, family, area, or industry.

When I think about being an impact leader, I think BIG. I want to invite you to think big with me for a moment. Let's start by taking a look at one of the most impactful leaders of all time: Jesus of Nazareth. Regardless of your stance on Jesus, it's evident that His story stands the test of time—far greater than that of any other historical figure.

HISTORICAL EVIDENCE: JESUS & HIS IMPACT

Here are a few examples to highlight the lasting impact of Jesus on the world as we know it today:

Jesus lived over 2,000 years ago, yet his teachings are still central to modern global culture, ethics, and religious thought. This shows that His impact wasn't temporary and that His approach was clearly timeless. When I think about the impact I want to have, I want it to be long-lasting, not just temporary. Some call this a legacy; I call it a life worth living.

The Bible, which centers on Jesus' life and teachings, remains the most widely distributed and most translated book in human history. There are over 2.4 billion Christians (or followers of Jesus Christ) worldwide.

Source: Pew Research Center (2023)

This makes Christianity the largest religion in the world, encompassing over 31% of the global population. In other words, there is no person in the world who is followed more readily than Jesus. Talk about being a leader who has an impact. In addition, Christianity spans every inhabited continent and has followers in nearly every nation on Earth. This shows that His impact wasn't limited to a single geographic area.

Over 5 billion copies of the Bible have been distributed. Source: Guinness World Records

Portions of the Bible have been translated into more than 3,600 languages, with the New Testament available in over 1,500. Source: Wycliffe Global Alliance (2023)

This begs the next question: How can I have an impact that spans borders, languages, and cultures?

Still not convinced about the impact of Jesus? This blew my mind... The Gregorian calendar, used by most of the world, is based on the birth of Jesus (AD/BC). Even secular or non-Christian cultures often use this system, signifying His influence on how the world marks time. This tells me that His life had to be important if most of the world uses it as a reference to measure and track time.

Just when I thought His influence must be running out, I found out that the first hospitals, universities, and charities were founded by Christians in Jesus' name. Some notable universities and charities influenced by Jesus in modern society include: Oxford, Cambridge, Harvard, Yale, the Red Cross, World Vision, and Doctors Without Borders.

Jesus' emphasis on servanthood, compassion, and the value of every individual helped shape Western concepts of human rights, dignity, and justice. One foundational ethic in many legal systems and moral philosophies today is the Golden Rule ("Do unto others as you would have them do unto you" – Luke 6:31), first taught by Jesus 2,000 years ago. His impact is woven throughout society everywhere.

These are just a few examples. Now you begin to see a fuller picture of the lasting impact of Jesus on global society as we know it today.

Now that we've seen the massive impact Jesus has had on this earth, let's take a look at *how* He was able to make such an impact in such a short time here on this earth (remember—He only lived thirty-three years, and only did ministry for three of those years). Accomplishing all of this in such a short time tells me that He was very intentional with everything that He did. We should be also. I believe His unparalleled impact is marked by a few key traits:

1. Serving Others Selflessly (John 13:3-5)
2. Loving Others Limitlessly (Luke 23:34, John 15:13)
3. Elevating Others Endlessly (Matthew 4:18-19 and 16:18)
4. Implementing a Lifestyle of Integrity (Matthew 6:5)
5. Maintaining Your Mission (Matthew 28:19-20 and 22:37-39, 1 John 4:19)

Let's dive deeper into these traits.

1. Jesus represented the greatest act of serving others by washing their feet. This includes washing the feet of the person He knew would soon betray him (and have him killed). Do you want to have a lasting impact? Get others-focused. Serve them with no expectation of getting anything in return—even those who mean you harm.

2. Jesus loves others so much that He was willing to die for them (sacrificial love). This includes the ones who wrongfully killed him. You see, it wasn't enough for Him to love those who loved him or those who "deserved it," because that's what most people do. He loves everybody, even the people who murdered him. This separates Him from others who love conditionally or when it is convenient for them.

3. This may seem pretty intuitive, but to be a leader, you have to have people following you. However, to be an impact leader, you have to elevate the people following you. The only way a leader can truly make an impact is by empowering the people under them to make an impact. The more you elevate others, the more impact you'll have. We see this in the Bible, where Jesus empowered ordinary people to become leaders in His mission and, eventually, in the church.

4. Nobody likes a hypocrite. To have real impact, you must practice what you preach. What you do when nobody is looking is equally as important, if not more important, than what you do when others are paying attention. Jesus rebuked the hypocrites and lived exactly how He taught others to live. This makes it much easier to maintain a platform of impact. Your character must be able to maintain the platform you're speaking from (whether your talents got you to where you are, or the platform has been handed to you).

5. Don't get distracted. You have to be intentional about the steps you take to achieve your mission. When the going gets rough, remember why you started in the first place. Jesus Himself modeled this resolve—sweating blood in the garden of Gethsemane, fully aware of what would come next. Yet He was so committed to His mission that He willingly went to the cross, paying the ultimate price by giving His life to fulfill it. To be on-mission doesn't mean you never slow down; it means you have a guiding light you're always striving toward, keeping you headed in the right direction. What separates impact leaders from others is their willingness and discipline to persist through the ups and downs, fueled by their ability to remember their why.

HOW HIS IMPACT HAS TRANSFORMED ME

When I studied Jesus' life and reflected on these traits, I decided the best way to make a lasting impact and lead a life of significance would be to practice them. I began to incorporate them into all aspects of my life. Over time, I started to see favor in my life that had never existed previously. Some may call it luck; I call it grace. This became a walking testimony for me.

As soon as I started leading like Jesus, the impact inevitably followed. Impact followed because while I practiced these traits, they *actually* began to change me as a person. I started seeing the good in people when I used to see only bad; opportunities when I used to see obstacles; and blessings instead of tragedies. This new person I became attracted others and allowed me to point them toward significance. Naturally, I became a leader with growing impact.

In this season, I learned some very important lessons. I quickly realized life wasn't all about me and my own desires. If you can make the shift from life being about you to life being about others, then you'll truly be able to lead a life of impact. I have come to understand that we, as humans, all seek something more than what we can see or touch. While our method of choice for that search varies, only one path leads you to a life of impact.

HOW I'VE IMPACTED OTHERS:
PICKING UP MY CROSS & CARRYING IT

When I look at my life now, I see many opportunities to lead a life of impact: in my business, in my family, in my friends, in my community, and (I'm going to think BIG again) globally.

When I look at the five traits I mentioned earlier, I can see how I've consistently incorporated them into my life. From serving (1) my church to loving (2) our clients, to elevating (3) my employees, to implementing integrity (4) by doing the same things behind closed doors as in the public, all the way to sticking with my mission (5) to be an impact leader.

Are you called to be an impact leader? I would posit that if you're reading this book, the answer to that question would be **YES**!

So, what's holding you back? Start leading a life of impact today!

- Serve Others Selflessly

- Love Others Limitlessly

- Elevate Others Endlessly

- Implement a Lifestyle of Integrity

- Maintain Your Mission

It's the small, daily decisions you make that will create true transformation in your life. I'll leave you with one piece of inspiration. My mother used to tell me every night before bed, "Be the best person you can be." She told me this daily so I would remember that it was a daily decision, followed by daily actions. I realize now that this was her way of creating an impact leader out of me.

When you not only practice these traits but also allow them to become part of who you are, you step into the life of an impact leader.

SPENCE TRICK

Spence Trick is a world-renowned wakesurfing coach and the owner of Wakesurf Tampa, a premier watersports charter company in Tampa Bay, Florida. Growing up on a lake in northern Indiana, his love for wakesports began early and later inspired him to found the Wakesports Club at the University of Alabama.

With a background in Mechanical Engineering, Spence combines an analytical approach with a passion for teaching, breaking down complex skills into simple, accessible steps. While his coaching has helped countless people excel on the water, his mission extends far beyond wakesurfing.

Transformed by his faith in Jesus Christ, Spence is devoted to helping others live with purpose, integrity, and impact. He leads the Young Adults ministry and multiple small groups at Radiant Church, encouraging people to embrace their calling and unique strengths. His message is clear: true success is not measured by accolades but by living intentionally, serving others, and finding joy and fulfillment in a life of purpose.

Through his coaching, leadership, and ministry, Spence continues to inspire people to unlock their potential—on the water, in their careers, and in their communities.

www.WakeSurfTampaBay.com
LinkedIn: *www.linkedin.com/in/Spence-Trick*

FINAL WORDS

As we turn the final page of this book, I hope you don't see it as an ending—but as the beginning of something far greater.

The stories you've just read are not just about success. They are stories of courage. Of resilience. Of people who chose to rise, again and again, not just for themselves, but for the lives they could touch along the way.

Leadership isn't always about titles or stages or even accomplishments. Leadership is about impact. It's about being bold enough to turn your pain into purpose. Brave enough to speak your truth out loud. And grounded enough to lift others as you climb.

Each of the authors featured in *The Impact Leaders* carries a vision, a mission, and a message that will echo long beyond their time on this earth. That's what impact is. It's the footprint we leave—not in sand, but in people. It's the ripple we start with a single act of service, courage, or love.

You don't have to be famous to be remembered. You don't have to be perfect to make a difference. You just have to be willing to show up —fully, authentically, and fearlessly—as who you really are.

If this book has reminded you of one thing, let it be this:

Your story matters. Your voice matters. And your leadership— when rooted in truth and purpose—can change everything.

So, go lead boldly. Build something that outlives you. Make your mark not just with what you do, but with who you become in the process.

This is your legacy.

With all my heart,

Nim Stant
Founder, International Impact Book Awards
Creator of *The Impact Leaders*

250